A BIBLIOGRAPHY OF HARVEY CUSHING

American Association of Neurological Surgeons

Harvey Cushing

April 8, 1869–October 7, 1939

Ave atque vale

A BIBLIOGRAPHY OF THE WRITINGS OF
HARVEY CUSHING

PREPARED ON THE OCCASION OF HIS
SEVENTIETH BIRTHDAY APRIL 8, 1939
BY THE HARVEY CUSHING SOCIETY

Third Edition
(Revised 1993)

AMERICAN ASSOCIATION OF NEUROLOGICAL SURGEONS

Rolling Meadows, Illinois

Linda S. Miller, AANS Staff Editor

The text of *A Bibliography of the Writings of Harvey Cushing (Third
Edition)* was printed on Crosspointe Bellbrook Laid Oxford Cream
paper, a similar paper as that of the first 2 editions. The type font
in the third edition is Cushing Book—a derivative of the same type
font used in the first 2 editions which was created by a distant
relative of Harvey Cushing.

CONTENTS

Page

FOREWORD

THE present compilation includes all of Dr. Cushing's published writings that could be traced through the usual bibliographical channels. The first section sets forth his degrees and titles, the second his books and monographs, and the third is a chronological list of his contributions to periodicals extending over a period of an even forty years; the final section is an alphabetical list of papers which have emanated from Dr. Cushing's Laboratories and Clinics. The section on books contains 14 separate titles, with a total of 25 entries, including separate editions and translations; in the list of journal contributions 309 titles are represented; and, finally, 330 papers have been cited that Dr. Cushing has himself encouraged or directed. In offering this bibliography to him on his birthday, we do so in the hope that his extraordinary productivity may long continue, and that, by making his writings more readily available, others may derive the enduring inspiration that we have had from his precept and example.

The Society takes this opportunity of expressing its gratitude to Mr. Carl Purington Rollins, Printer to Yale University, for the time and attention he has given to designing the bibliography. It will no doubt interest readers to learn that the type face, well known to typographers as "Cushing No. 25," was originally introduced by Josiah Stearns Cushing, a distant kinsman of Harvey Cushing. To the George Banta Publishing Company which has printed the bibliography, and to Mr. Charles C Thomas who will publish it, the Society is also greatly indebted.

April 8, 1939   THE SOCIETY

NOTE TO SECOND EDITION

In the new edition corrections have been made with additions covering the interval between February 1939 and the time of Dr. Cushing's death on October 7, 1939.

Feb. 1, 1940   THE SOCIETY

INTRODUCTION TO THE THIRD EDITION

This slim volume presents an annotated checklist of the written works of Dr. Harvey Cushing, presented to him on his 70th birthday in 1939, only a few months before his death. It covers a career span of 45 years: his 10 years in general surgery, 28 years as an operating neurosurgeon, and 7 years in retirement. His literary output was huge, numbering 15 books and monographs and over 300 addresses, papers in journals, and reports, and it embraced literature for the layman as well as for the scientist. Writing during evenings at home, he researched his subjects exhaustively and often brought unknown incidents to light for an audience of supposed savants. He was versatile and while he never attempted to write a murder mystery, I am sure that had he done so, it would have been a good one.

Cushing was not an easy writer in the manner of Abraham Lincoln, who is said to have composed his Gettysburg Address while riding the train to the battlefield, nor did he have the facility of his friend William H. Welch, who wrote his hour-long "Ether Day Address" for delivery at the Massachusetts General Hospital in the noisy men's lavatory of a Pullman car on the way to Boston. Cushing would worry through 5 or 6 revisions of a manuscript in his attempt to improve it right up to the moment when it went to the printer, and sometimes even after type was set.

Edward Weeks, editor of the *Atlantic Monthly Press*, tells us what it was like to edit a Cushing book[1]: "We had accepted for publication a collection of Dr. Cushing's papers; the book was to be called *Consecratio Medici*[2] and it was my responsibility to see the manuscript through the press, to check the Doctor's corrections, learn his preferences for the binding and jacket and to make sure that there was nothing to offend him in the blurb. He took the proofreading very seriously, had an eye like a hawk for printers' errors or a loose line, and made meticulous corrections, first in the galleys, and then in the page proofs. Nothing escaped him. I had heard that he was a perfectionist and, in his taut, decisive way, intimidating; now I knew it."

That was in 1928. Six years later, after Cushing had retired and moved to New Haven, Edward Weeks handled a far more difficult task, that of bringing to press Cushing's wartime journals.[3] His account of this period puts us in awe of Cushing as a writer.

"On January 20 I made my initial visit to the big house on Whitney Avenue where I was installed with the journal in a little

---

[1]*In Friendly Candor, Atlantic Monthly Press,* Little, Brown and Company, Boston, 1959.
[2]*Consecratio Medici and Other Papers,* Little, Brown and Company, Boston, 1928.
[3]*From a Surgeon's Journal 1915–1918.* Boston, Little, Brown and Company, 1936.

sun porch off the living room. Fourteen months later, after eleven
visits and the exchange of 113 letters, *From a Surgeon's Journal*
came off the press. The manuscript had grown from 45,000 to
190,000 words. Not a sentence was rewritten; my editorial touch
was needed only in the preparation of an Introduction and
Afterword—and here Harvey edited me. Caring for Cushing as an
author was a full-time occupation: the enormous correspondence,
the give and take which engrossed us and our secretaries, was
concerned, fastidiously and impatiently, with questions of propri-
ety, typography, punctuation, illustration, capitalization, maps and
libel. As the book grew, the royalty terms which he demanded
rose; the contract was renegotiated three times; he never would
accept the libel clause; and midway in the manufacture he obliged
us to discard all galleys in the original type face and reset the
entire text in a format more closely resembling a diary."

The reader fortunately does not have to suffer through the
birthing pains of Cushing's numerous literary progeny, since this
chore fell to his patient secretary, Madeline Stanton, who typed
immaculately while quietly correcting his spelling errors to bring
forth some of medicine's finest writings.

The Cushing legacy offers a feast of delicacies. While his early
reports are concerned with technical matters, in 1901 he
relaxed enough to report from Europe on "Haller and his
native town", the first indication of his interest in medical history.
In 1906, there came forth the fascinating and immensely appealing
"Dr. Garth: the Kit-Kat Poet (1661–1718)" and "The holders of the
gold-headed cane as book collectors", the latter foretelling his own
attraction to rare books. Although he was intrigued by the book
collecting of the successive holders of the gold-headed cane, who
were the medical elite of London in the days of Marlborough and
Walpole, Cushing's chief interest lay in "The quatercentenary of
Andreas Vesalius, 1514–1914", for he was soon to be locked into
what became a lifelong search for the various editions and piracies
of the famous 16th century anatomist, which culminated in his
book, published posthumously, "The Bio-bibliography of Andreas
Vesalius".[4]

We pass over the wartime years and move on to the final period. Returning from France in February, 1919, Cushing set out
upon an uninterrupted 13 years of work as a surgeon, as an international figure ("The most influential man in the medical world"—
Welch), and as one of the most sought-after speakers in medical
academe, for his growing fame brought heavy demands upon his

---

*The librarian at Yale Medical School informs us that a new edition of this will be pub-
lished in the near future by Norman Publishing.

time, and he had an impressive stage presence, an engaging personality. In 1921 and following, we find him giving the luncheon address to his 30th class reunion at Yale; entertaining the Ether Day audience of the Massachusetts General Hospital with "The personality of a hospital"; and delivering his presidential address to the annual meeting of the American College of Surgeons on "The physician and the surgeon". Next he awarded the Henry Jacob Bigelow medal to the venerable W.W. Keen; spoke on "Laboratories: then and now" at the opening of the Biological Building at McGill; travelled to Baltimore to honor medicine's indebtedness to the nursing profession with a talk on "Louisa Parsons"; praised the women of the New England Surgical Dressing Committee with the "Boston Tins"; spoke as President of the American Neurological Association on his own personal experiences; gave one of his finest historical essays on "The Western Reserve and its medical traditions" at Cleveland where he grew up in the medical environment of a doctor father and a doctor grandfather. Off to Yale to dedicate the Sterling Hall of Medicine; to Philadelphia for his "Consecratio medici", back to Cleveland for "The doctor and his books", and to Dartmouth to give the students his philosophy on "The medical career". He opened the new Welch Library at Johns Hopkins with a splendid address on "The binding influence of a library on a subdividing profession"; celebrated the sesquicentennial of the Massachusetts Medical Society with "One hundred and fifty years. From tallow-dip to television", and reminisced on "Homo chirurgicus" for the Boston Surgical Society. Even in retirement we find him in Washington speaking on "Medicine at the crossroads"; driving to a northwestern Connecticut graveside to eulogize his friend with the memorable speech, "The Doctors Welch of Norfolk"; to Syracuse with another historical paper on "The pioneer medical schools of Central New York"; honoring his duties as the president of the History of Science Society with apt reflections on "The humanizing of science"; re-telling the story of "William Beaumont's rendezvous with fame" at a highway dedication in Connecticut, and reviewing a once popular anatomical drawing called the *écorché*, which is the picture of the body with the skin taken off, with "Ercole Lelli and his écorché" before the American Association for the Advancement of Science in Atlantic City. In reciting these events we have covered only his major addresses in America, but he was equally popular in Europe as we can see by a glance at the section on "Vita, Degrees and Honors" in this volume. Honorary degrees, fellowships, and medals were showered upon him and most of them required substantial responses.

His crowning literary achievement was the "Life of Sir William Osler", a monumental biography in 2 volumes of about 700 pages each, which occupied him from 1921 until publication in 1925, and won for him the Pulitzer Prize in Letters.

We are fortunate that so many of his essays are available to us today through the library system. Cushing was an inspiring teacher, and on reading his works one feels the intimacy of sitting beside him, perhaps in his study at 305 Walnut Street in Brookline with the family's cocker spaniel curled up at his feet. He was especially effective on a one-to-one basis, a never-to-be-forgotten experience to those of us lucky enough to have enjoyed this privilege. On a sudden whim he would drop everything to help a junior house officer dress up his first scientific paper for publication, or show a promising student through the Boston Medical Library, or guide a young colleague through the great Shakespearean collection in the Folger Library in Washington—and he seemed to be at his happiest when doing these things.

When we turn to his professional papers, which comprise about 90% of the collection, we have time only to point to broad trends. For example, when he decided to confine his practice to neurosurgery in 1905, he first summarized the state of the art in "The special field of neurological surgery", and updated this report in 1910 and again in 1920. During the final years, working exclusively with brain tumors, his reports deal with *types of tumors* such as meningiomas, acoustic neuromas, hemangiomas, medulloblastomas, and of course, pituitary tumors, which became his favorite subject. Finally, in 1931 he wrapped it all up with "The surgical mortality percentages pertaining to a series of two thousand verified intracranial tumors" which he read before the First International Neurological Congress in Berne, Switzerland, closing his remarks with a statement that brought the crowded auditorium to a hushed silence: "Gentlemen," he said "this will be the last report on the statistical results of brain tumors as a whole that I shall ever publish."

Appraising Cushing's position in medical history is like trying to catch hold of a fast moving train, for Cushing was part of a rapidly changing landscape of medical scenery, and one has to feel the sense of motion to understand the man.

At the start, however, he got on the wrong train, a pokey little trolley car that circled around Boston's medical horizon, seldom venturing beyond the confines of the Charles River Basin. It was called the Massachusetts General Hospital. J.M.T. Finney tells what it was like in 1889: "Much of the surgery was done in a dense fog of carbolic spray. While the surgeon washed his hands with soap and water and rinsed them in bichloride or carbolic acid solution he then donned a black Prince Albert coat which was covered with spots of blood and pus left by many an earlier operation, for these coats were seldom cleaned. No wonder suppurating wounds and drainage tubes were the order of the day.[5] And 7 years later Cushing, standing in Finney's shoes as an M.G.H. intern, wrote in his diary "Not operating much. Considerable sepsis in the house. No wonder, these men operate about the way a commercial traveler grabs breakfast at a lunch counter."

(The writer was present in 1929 when the Medical Examiner of Suffolk County [Boston] came to Dr. Cushing's home one evening— he was too embarrassed to make an office call—to seek help for his dreadfully deformed hands, which had suffered multiple infections from doing surgical autopsies bare-handed, a tradition that he stubbornly refused to give up!!)

Meanwhile, down in Baltimore, creative scientists had been working on a new kind of train, one that was different from anything ever seen before, and had assembled a phenomenal crew to run it. Welch was to be the engineer, Osler the fireman, Halsted the repairman, and Kelly the timekeeper. They were all young, in their thirties; they had grown up in the rough and tumble environment of crowded charity hospitals; their viewpoints had been broadened and sharpened by years of study in the noted laboratories of Europe; and they were free from the overbearing handicap of tradition; *indeed, they were urged to break with the past and to build a new medical world.* When on May 7, 1889, this strange new vehicle boarded its first passengers and moved smoothly out of the antiquated shed of the past, this medical equivalent of "Le Train à la Grande Vitesse" of France set out to do just that.

The passage of time has enshrined these men in our medical halls of fame to recall for us how Welch masterminded the nation's preventive measures against disease so well that President Hoover hailed him as "our greatest statesman of Public Health"; how Osler challenged the therapeutic practices of centuries past with his revolutionary "Principles and Practice of Medicine"; how Halsted through 12 years of laboratory experimentation single-handedly converted surgery from the half-way stage of antisepsis to the final, ultimate triumph of asepsis that we know today. The Johns Hopkins Hospital was so far ahead of its time that when Cushing left Boston in 1896 to enter Halsted's surgical service in Baltimore, it was like jumping straight out of the nineteenth century into the twentieth.

---

[5]Crowe, S.J. *Halsted of Johns Hopkins.* Charles C Thomas, 1957.

It is said that great things happen when Preparedness meets Opportunity and the allusion is most apt in Cushing's case. Ten years of general surgery under Halsted had prepared him for any special field of surgery that he might wish to choose, and the opportunity most appealing to his competitive nature was surgery of the brain with its dismal mortality rate of above 70%. He set out to correct this and had the tools with which to do it: inexhaustible energy, unbridled ambition, the athlete's compulsion to win, and the artist's eye for perfection.

Cushing did not invent neurosurgery, but he made it happen. He showed that when Halsted's rules of surgery were followed—the gentle handling of tissue, the use of fine silk for ligature and suture, preservation of blood supply, closure in layers without tension—that surgery of the brain was little different from surgery of any other region of the body. He was later to explain it in this way: "An entire change in the character of operative workmanship largely explains the transformation in the surgery of the past decade or two.... Observers no longer expect to be thrilled in an operating room; the spectacular public performances of the past, no longer condoned, are replaced by the quiet, rather tedious procedures which few beyond the operator, his assistants, and the immediate bystanders can profitably see. The patient on the table, like the passenger in a car, runs great risks if he has a loquacious driver, or one who takes close corners, exceeds the speed limit, or rides to applause."[6] Finally, having turned neurosurgery into a viable specialty, he peopled it with over 80 of his trainees and became its most eloquent spokesman.

Time dulls our memories, and the Cushing era of almost a century ago lies largely forgotten by today's neurosurgeons, the majority of whom were not even born at the time of his death in 1939. It is to keep his memory alive that this book is being reprinted by the Association so that present and future members may come to know their vocational ancestor through the vehicle of his writings. Art *is* long and Life *is* short, but not too short to pursue, as Cushing did, the by-ways of medicine, and there are few better ways of filling in the hours of our lengthening life span, those hours given to us by these very men, than to study their lives.

RICHARD U. LIGHT, M.D.
speaking for that Once and
Future Institution, the
Harvey Cushing Society

[6]*Realignments in greater medicine.* Address given at the Seventeenth International Congress of Medicine, London, 1913.

BIBLIOGRAPHIA ANIMATA

WHAT is the most fitting way of celebrating a birth-day anniversary? Can anything take the place of the cake with the appropriate number of candles plus one to grow on, and the shiny dime hidden deep in its inside? When one has watched so many radiant faces of birthday children before the blazing cake, the raptured gazes that followed the knife plunging into the crackling frosting and the joyous hunt for the secreted dime, it does not seem that anything can replace the cake. Alas the time comes when a reasonably sized cake cannot hold the number of candles required, and although the ideal of mass production has invaded the candlestick maker's art, the little tapers it furnishes have serious inconveniences. When some decades ago my own child provided me lovingly with one, I felt in the fierce blaze like one thrown into purgatory rather than lifted into the "deep domed empyrean" of paternal felicity. It is a barbaric custom anyway, this keeping track, numerically, of one's years; only a childlike spirit can redeem it.

We who are supposed to have outgrown childhood, or at least childishness, and especially we of a profession which must preserve a certain dignity, we have found a substitute in a symbolical birthday cake, the *Festschrift*. This name—there is no very good translation—shows that the idea is an imported one, and for that reason if for no other, we avoid it in these days of national self-sufficiency. And anyway it is an uneatable, indigestible concoction of many cooks who fail to harmonize what each provides, towards a tempting palatable cake. An example, the two volumes that were presented to Osler, *aet*.LXX, two birthday cakes really, the one hundred and forty-two contributions providing the requisite number of candles, plus one each "to grow on." One wonders if he, this great lover of children, noticed this curious adherence to the birthday cake principle. One feels sure that it would have enhanced his enjoyment, for a childlike spirit was in him to the last.

Dr. Welch at eighty was presented with a fine collection of *éloges* and with a very appropriate account of all the many luncheons and dinners held in his honor in this country and all around the world. This latter aspect of this eloquent homage shows that also here an adherence to the birthday cake principle was attained. Probably this was not the least appeal it made to him. It gave him the chance to be one of

that gathering of choice and devoted spirits around an im-
mense board. Wasn't it the intimate personal contact that
allowed him to achieve the great things he did? More difficult
it was to respond appropriately to the *éloges*. He said simply:
"I must speak in my own person and not in that of the ideal-
ized figure which has been presented to you."

Here is a hint about what an ideal birthday cake might
be: gather what he said in his own person, put it out neatly
and nicely in the proper sequence, and with the accents
placed where they belong, not a *catalogue raisonné,* but a
humanized bibliography. The proposition when made struck
me as a most happy one, and he who made it being a master
chef in this matter, I already visioned and tasted, not only
the present, but the ultimate product. No *opera omnia* are
envisaged. These no doubt, and alas, will come some day,
but these expansive tributes, unless based on a sympatheti-
cally pondered bibliography, usually have only the weight
of elaborate tombstones. Bibliography, like *Pagliaccio* in the
old Italian theatre, draws the curtains apart and wistfully tells
the audience what is to come, of the great chief in his science
and art, of the healer of the hopeless, the teacher and his
boys, the comrade in peace and war, the man who seeks and
sees the funny side of all things, one who in the teeth of toil,
strife and heavy responsibility preserved a youthful and lov-
able spirit that still infuses every one of his many pupils
around the world.

An outlook on all this, bibliography would appear to many
to open but a very narrow door. This is true for many cases,
in others the failure is the reader's who has not learned to read
it. But it is becoming more and more a fine art. To eyes that
know how to see, it presents a sort of cardiogram of a writer,
recording not only the single beats, like the colors assembled on a painter's palette or the scales of tones ready
for evocation in the musician's instrument. But not only
this but those subtle fusions of values, what the Greeks
called τριβὴ μετὰ λόγου, which alone could make the master-
piece or picture the inner life of a writer. The bibliographer
will not only consider the facts, the titles, but their intervals,
he will feel and find the causes that determined certain
things to be written and why others apparently needed were
not written. And lucky it is when the writer is still there to
make discoveries in his own work long forgotten though still
fresh in meaning.

Singularly rich will be this harvest. One not fully satisfied
with the "surface washings" of the anatomist, went "digging

deep for gold" for "novelties and chance findings," deep into
the hormonal regions with glimpses into still deeper worlds of
molecules, atoms, protons, electrons . . . adapting, shaping
with Edisonian inventiveness the indispensable tools. With
Dr. Holyoke of Salem from "Tallow-dip to Television"
scanning the historical horizon, with ponderous Dr. Haller
not talking only Latin but genuine Bärndütsch, disporting
himself humorously and revealingly in Sir Samuel Garth's
Dispensary, and without end in green Vesalian fields picking
the choicest flowers here and there. And crowning it all in
that *Life of Osler,* the happiest fusion of the objective and
subjective that biographical art has ever turned out in our
rich literature.

With all these fine materials it ought to make a wonderful
birthday cake. Bon appétit!

> Grand vieillard, de l'année entière
> Vous ne prenez que le printemps:
> Vous n'êtes pas septuagénaire,
> Vous avez sept fois dix ans!

ARNOLD C. KLEBS

NOTES FOR THE THIRD EDITION

CUSHING'S PUBLICATIONS PRINTED SINCE 1940*

Consecratio medici, and other papers, by Harvey Cushing. Boston: Little, Brown and Company, 1940. [Republication; see No. 15.]

The Life of Sir William Osler, by Harvey Cushing. London and New York: Oxford University Press, 1940. (Originally published in 1925 in two volumes) [Republication; see No. 6.]

24b. *A Bio-bibliography of Andreas Vesalius,* by Harvey Cushing. New York: Schuman's, 1943. Edited by John F. Fulton. Published posthumously.

Yale University. School of Medicine. Yale Medical Library. Historical Library. The Harvey Cushing collection of books and manuscripts. New York: Schuman's, 1943.

24c. *A Visit to Le Puy-en-Velay, an Illustrated Diary by Harvey Cushing.* Cleveland, Ohio: The Rowfant Club, 1944. Published posthumously. Republished in 1986. Limited edition (1986) available from the American Association of Neurological Surgeons, Park Ridge, Illinois.

A Bio-Bibliography of Andreas Vesalius, 2nd Edition. Hamden, NJ: CT Archon Books, 1962. [Republication; see No. 24b above.]

Meningiomas: Their Classification, Regional Behavior, Life History, and Surgical Results. With collaboration of Louise Eisenhardt, New York: Hafner Publishing Company, 1962. [Republication; see No. 24.]

Tumors of the Nervus Acusticus and the Syndrome of the Cerebellopontile Angle. New York: Hafner Publishing Company, 1963. [Republication; see No. 3.]

---

*This bibliography of the posthumous publications of Harvey Cushing's works was provided by Ferenc Gyorgyey, Historical Librarian at Yale University's Harvey Cushing/John Hay Whitney Medical Library.

THE CUSHING CHRONOLOGY

Harvey Cushing graduated from Yale in 1891, from the Harvard Medical School in 1895, served a year as a House Pupil at the Massachusetts General Hospital, then switched to Baltimore to move upward through a four-year residency program in surgery under Halsted. Following a year in Europe, he returned to Baltimore as an Assistant Professor of Surgery, staying there until 1912 when he moved to full professorship at Harvard. He retired in 1932, and accepted Yale's offer of a Sterling Professorship in Neurology, which he held nearly until his death in 1939 at the age of 70.

I. DR. HARVEY CUSHING
VITA, DEGREES AND HONORS

HARVEY CUSHING: VITA, DEGREES AND HONORS

ORN in Cleveland, Ohio, April 8, 1869. Brother of Edward F. Cushing (1862–1911), M.D. (Harvard), late Professor of Pediatrics, Western Reserve Medical School; son of Henry K. Cushing (1827–1910), M.D. (Univ. of Penn.), LL.D., formerly Professor of Obstetrics and Gynaecology, Western Reserve Medical School; grandson of Erastus Cushing (1802–1893), M.D. (Berkshire Medical Institution); great-grandson of Dr. David Cushing, Jr. (1768–1814) of Cheshire, Massachusetts. Died in New Haven, Connecticut, October 7, 1939.

Bachelor of Arts, Yale, 1891.
Doctor of Medicine, Master of Arts, Harvard, 1895.
House Officer, Massachusetts General Hospital, 1895–1896.
Johns Hopkins Hospital and Medical School, 1896–1900.
  Assistant Resident Surgeon, October 1896–October 1897.
  Resident Surgeon, October 1897–May 1900.
  Instructor in Surgery, 1897–1898.
  Assistant in Surgery, 1898–1899.
  Associate in Surgery, 1899–1900.
Student under Theodor Kocher and Hugo Kronecker (Bern) and Charles S. Sherrington (Liverpool), 1900–1901.
Johns Hopkins Hospital and Medical School, 1901–1912.
  Associate in Surgery, March 1902–September 1912.
  Associate Professor of Surgery, 1903–1912.
Harvard University Medical School, Moseley Professor of Surgery, 1912–1932; Professor Emeritus, 1932–1939.
Surgeon-in-Chief, Peter Bent Brigham Hospital, 1912–1932; Surgeon-in-Chief Emeritus, 1932–1939.
Director, U. S. Army Base Hospital No. 5, 1917–1919.
Senior Consultant in Neurological Surgery, A. E. F., 1918.
Yale University, Sterling Professor of Neurology, 1933–1937; Professor Emeritus, 1937–1939; Director of Studies in the History of Medicine, School of Medicine, 1937–1939. Associate Fellow, Trumbull College, 1933–1939.
Consulting Neurologist, New Haven Hospital, 1933–1939.

1900
Member, American Association of Pathologists and Bacteriologists

1901
Mütter Lecturer (Philadelphia)

1902
Member, American Association for the Advancement of Science

1903
Member, American Neurological Association (President, 1923)
Charter member, American Society of Clinical Surgery (President, 1921)

1905
Member, American Physiological Society

3

1906
Fellow, American Surgical Association (President, 1927)
Wesley M. Carpenter Lecturer (New York)

1909
William Mitchell Banks Memorial Lecturer (University of Liverpool)
Member, Royal Medical Society of Budapest

1910
Harvey Society Lecturer (New York)

1913
Master of Arts (Hon.), Yale
Orator in Surgery, XVIIth International Congress of Medicine (London)
Fellow (Hon.), Royal College of Surgeons, England
Fellow (Hon.), Institute of Hygiene (London)
Fellow, American College of Surgeons (President, 1922)

1914
Weir Mitchell Lecturer (Philadelphia)
Foreign corresponding member, Société de Neurologie, Paris
Fellow, American Academy of Arts and Sciences
Member, Washington Academy of Sciences

1915
Doctor of Science, Washington University (Mo.)

1917
Member, National Academy of Sciences
Fellow, Societas Medicorum Svecana

1918
Fellow, Royal College of Surgeons (Ireland)

1919
Honorary Fellow, American Psychiatric Association
Doctor of Laws, Western Reserve University
Doctor of Science, Yale University
Companion of the Bath (Military)
Doctor of Medicine (Hon.), Queen's University, Belfast
Membre associé, Société Royale des Sciences Médicales et Naturelles
de Bruxelles
Membre associé étranger, Société Nationale de Chirurgie, Paris

1920
Charter member, Society of Neurological Surgeons (President, 1920
and 1921)
Doctor of Laws, University of Cambridge
Corresponding member, Société de Biologie, Paris

1921
Honorary Fellow, Medical Society of London (Orator, 1927)
Corresponding member, Gesellschaft der Aerzte in Wien (Ehrenmit-
glied, 1932)

1922

Charles Mickle Fellow, University of Toronto
Cavendish Lecturer (London)
Perpetual Student (Hon.), St. Bartholomew's Hospital, London
Chevalier, Légion d'Honneur
Corresponding member, Medico-Chirurgical Society, Edinburgh

1923

United States Distinguished Service Medal
Correspondant étranger 2° Division, Académie de Médecine, Paris
Fellow (Hon.), Association of Surgeons of Great Britain and Ireland

1924

Cameron Prize Lecturer (University of Edinburgh)
Corresponding member, Società Medico-Chirurgica di Bologna

1925

Honorary Fellow, Cleveland Medical Library Association

1926

Member, Society of the New York Hospital
Doctor of Letters, Jefferson Medical College
Doctor of Medicine (Hon.), John Casimir University, Lwów, Poland
Pulitzer Prize in Letters, Columbia University
Honorary Fellow, New York Academy of Medicine

1927

Honorary Fellow, Royal Society of Medicine, London
Honorary Fellow, Royal Academy of Medicine in Ireland
Master of Surgery (Hon.), Trinity College, Dublin
Macewen Memorial Lecturer (University of Glasgow)
Doctor of Laws, University of Glasgow
Doctor of Laws, University of Edinburgh
Fellow (Hon.), Royal College of Surgeons, Edinburgh
Officier, Légion d'Honneur
Honorary member, Society of British Neurological Surgeons

1928

Foreign member, Societas Medica Havniensis (Honorary member, 1932)

1929

Foreign corresponding member, Société de Neurologie de Varsovie
Ehrenmitglied, Verein für Psychiatrie und Neurologie, Vienna
Honorary Fellow, Philadelphia Academy of Surgery
Arnold Knapp Prize in Ophthalmology, New York
Doctor of Letters, Dartmouth College
Associé étranger, Académie de Médecine, Paris
Lister Prize Medalist, Royal College of Surgeons, England
Order: El Sol del Perú
Honorary Fellow, American Medical Library Association
Corresponding member, Gesellschaft deutscher Nervenärzte (Ehren-
mitglied, 1933)
Docteur "honoris causa," University of Strasbourg
Corresponding member, Societas Regia Medicorum, Budapest

1930

Member, American Philosophical Society
Membre étranger (Hon.), Académie Royale de Médecine de Belgique
Honorary member, Royal Medico-Psychological Association, Great Britain
Docteur "honoris causa," University of Brussels
Award: Montclair Yale Bowl
Arthur Dean Bevan Lecturer, Chicago Surgical Society
Honorary member, Société Neurologique Estonienne
Membre associé étranger, Société Nationale de Chirurgie, Paris

1931

Docteur "honoris causa," University of Budapest
Donald Balfour Lecturer, University of Toronto
William H. Welch Lecturer, Mt. Sinai Hospital, New York
Honorary member, Beaumont Medical Club, New Haven
Foreign corresponding member, Società Piemontese di Chirurgia
Professor of History of Medicine, Johns Hopkins University (elect)
Doctor of Science, Harvard University
Doctor of Science, University of Rochester
Docteur "honoris causa," University of Bern

1932

Honorary member, Section of History of Medicine, Royal Society of Medicine, London
Mitglied, Kaiserliche Deutsche Akademie der Naturforscher
Doctor of Science, Northwestern University, Evanston-Chicago
Doctor of Medicine "honoris causa," University of Amsterdam (Tercentenary celebration)
Foreign corresponding member, British Medical Association
Foreign corresponding member, Sociedad Nacional de Cirugia de La Habana
Membro stranièro, Società Radio-Neuro-Chirurgica Italiana
Member, Royal Society of Sciences, Upsala
Honorary member, Società Italiana di Neurologia
Ehrenmitgleid, Gesellschaft deutscher Neurologen und Psychiater

1933

President, Congress of American Physicians and Surgeons
Harvey Society Lecturer (New York): second time
Honorary member, Pathological Society of Philadelphia (75th anniversary)
Honorary member, Hungarian Ophthalmological Society
Award: Henry Jacob Bigelow Medal, Boston Surgical Society
Docteur "honoris causa," University of Paris
Foreign member, Royal Society, London
Corresponding member, R. Accademia delle Scienze dell' Istituto di Bologna
Honorary member, North Caucasian Association of Neurologists and Psychiatrists
Honorary member, Norske Medicinske Selskab (100th jubilee)
Foreign corresponding member, Società Lombarda di Chirurgia
Honorary member, American Society of Regional Anesthesia
Award: "Golden Key," American Congress of Physical Therapy
Member, Societas Medica Norvegica

1934

Honorary foreign member, Société de Chirurgie de Lyon
Foreign member, Royal Academy of Sciences, Sweden
Doctor of Laws, Syracuse University (100th anniversary of Medical School)

1935

Honorary Fellow, Indian Academy of Sciences, Bangalore
Award: Gold medal, National Institute of Social Sciences
Foreign member, Royal Academy of Sciences, Amsterdam
Ehrenmitglied, Österreichische Gesellschaft für Erforschung und Bekämpfung der Krebskrankheit, Vienna
Honorary Fellow, Chicago Surgical Society
Doctor of Science, University of Leeds (*in absentia*)
Académico Honorario, Academia Nacional de Medicina de Buenos Aires
Honorary member, New York Neurological Society

1936

Associate member, Société de Biologie, Paris
Honorary member, Royal Medical Society, Edinburgh
Associé étranger, Académie de Chirurgie (previously Société Nationale de Chirurgie)
Ehrenmitglied, Gesellschaft der Chirurgen in Wien

1937

Ehrenmitglied, Wiener Biologische Gesellschaft

1938

Foreign corresponding member, Harveian Society of London
Foreign active member, Polish Academy of Science
Honorary member, American Ophthalmological Society
Doctor of Science "honoris causa," Oxford

1939

Corresponding member, Société Suisse de Neurologie
Honorary Fellow, Royal College of Physicians of London
Honorary member, Société d'Endocrinologie, Paris
Honorary Fellow, Royal Society of Edinburgh

II. BOOKS AND MONOGRAPHS

BOOKS AND MONOGRAPHS

I. PITUITARY BODY, 1912

1. The pituitary body and its disorders. Clinical states produced by disorders of the hypophysis cerebri. An amplification of the Harvey Lecture for December, 1910. *Philadelphia & London: J. B. Lippincott Co., 1912.* 8vo, colored frontispiece, x, 341 [3] pp. [319 numbered text figures; fig. 225 is a large folding plate inserted between pp. 166 and 167; last three pages blank].

❡This, Dr. Cushing's first separately published monograph, appeared late in 1911, the preface being dated September 11, 1911. The first printing (2000 copies) was sold within less than fifteen months; in this issue the author is described as follows: "Harvey Cushing, M.D. Associate Professor of Surgery the Johns Hopkins University Professor of Surgery (elect) Harvard University." In the second issue (1000 copies) the cancel title reads: "By Harvey Cushing, M.D. Moseley Professor of Surgery, Harvard University; Surgeon-in-Chief, the Peter Bent Bingham [*sic*] Hospital; formerly Associate Professor of Surgery, the Johns Hopkins University." Otherwise the title pages are the same. The second issue was also sold out promptly and the book has been out of print for nearly twenty years. The adjective "hypophysial" is misspelled "hypophyseal." The publishers refused to correct the spelling in the second issue with the result that until recently "hypophyseal" was given as the preferred spelling in Dorland's *The American Illustrated Medical Dictionary* (17th ed., 1936), and for a time was adopted as the official spelling by the editorial offices of the American Medical Association. After 1912 Dr. Cushing always spelled "hypophysial" with an "i" except when caused to use the "e" by the Journal office of the American Medical Association. *The pituitary body and its disorders* is the first clinical monograph on the hypophysis and it stands as one of the landmarks of modern endocrinology.

Dedication. The book is dedicated to his grandfather, father and brother as follows: "In loving memory of three physicians Erastus Cushing 1802–1893   Henry K. Cushing 1827–1910   Edward F. Cushing 1862–1911."

2. The same—second issue, also dated 1912, with cancel title page described in the preceding note; pagination unchanged.

II. TUMORS OF NERVUS ACUSTICUS, 1917

3. Tumors of the nervus acusticus and the syndrome of the cerebellopontile angle. *Philadelphia & London: W. B. Saunders Co., 1917.* 8vo, viii, 296 pp. [No frontispiece; 262 text figures; no inserts.]

❡The monograph on the acoustic neurinomas was prepared during the Great War and the manuscript was delivered to the printer just before

Dr. Cushing became Director of U. S. Army Base Hospital No. 5 in May 1917. The book was seen through the press by his assistant and collaborator, Dr. Louise Eisenhardt. The preface is dated "Boston, Mass., May 6, 1917." The section on surgical procedure with its well known illustrations of the cross-bow suboccipital approach was reprinted by the Surgeon-General in 1919 (No. 175 below). This monograph, of which 2500 copies were printed, was soon sold out; it was not issued separately in England and has not been reprinted save in the following French translation.
Dedication. "To my friend William T. Councilman."

4. Les tumeurs du nerf auditif et le syndrome de l'angle ponto-cérébelleux. Traduction française par les Docteurs Michel Deniker et Thierry de Martel. *Paris: Librairie Octave Doin, Gaston Doin, Éditeur, 1924.* 8vo, viii, 429 [3] pp.

⟨This translation, by two well known members of the French surgical profession, is complete and all 262 text figures are faithfully reproduced. The text is unchanged. The "Avertissement" (p. viii), signed "M.D. T. de M." is undated. It was issued bound and "broché"; the latter are in heavy undated orange covers reading: "Professeur Harwey [sic] Cushing / Tumeurs du Nerf Auditif / Traduction de M. Deniker & Th. de Martel / A Paris chez Gaston Doin—Editeur." Price 65 fr. broché.

III. STORY OF BASE HOSPITAL NO. 5, 1919

5. The story of U. S. Army Base Hospital No. 5. By a member of the Unit. *Cambridge, Mass.: University Press, 1919.* 8vo, halftone frontispiece inserted, 3 p.l., 118 pp., 19 unnumbered full-page halftone illustrations inserted facing pages 22, 30, 36, 38, 41, 44, 46, 48, 50, 52, 54, 56, 60 (folding), 66, 77, 92, 102, 108, 112.

⟨Signed anonymously "By a member of the Unit," this record covers the later as well as the antebellum period beginning in April 1915 when these volunteer units were first proposed. "The organization of these early volunteer Units was novel in that their members, drawn from the staff of a single institution and accustomed to work together, were likely to be more effective than a composite staff from several sources. This was brought to the attention of Surgeon-General Gorgas by Dr. Crile, and in the fall of 1915 he made a proposal to Dr. Crile and Dr. Cushing, both of whom were medical corps reserve officers, that they organize Units 'with the idea of doing the same work in some of our base hospitals in case of war, as was done in France' " (p. 5). The story is carried till January 1919 and pp. 77 to 118 contain a full roster of personnel including a list of publications (pp. 88–91). Some copies were bound in red and black; others in red covers (250 copies in all).

IV. LIFE OF SIR WILLIAM OSLER, 1925

6. The life of Sir William Osler. *Oxford: At the Clarendon Press, 1925.* 8vo, 2 vols., frontispiece, xvi, 685 [1] pp., 22

inserted and unnumbered collotype illustrations; frontispiece, xii, 728 pp., 22 inserted illustrations.

⟦This monumental account of his teacher and friend, Sir William Osler, was prepared beween the years 1921 and 1925, his earlier appreciations having been separately published (see No. 180 below). The manuscript originally extended to the equivalent of three volumes, but was extensively curtailed prior to publication. The first issue of 5000 copies was published April 16, 1925, and there have been three subsequent printings of 5000 each, so that 20,000 copies of this book have appeared; the Oxford Press states that the last printing is nearly exhausted. An eight-page list of errata, collected over a ten-year period, was issued by the Press in August 1936 (see below No. 324). Dr. Cushing has distributed these to those who have sent him corrections. Copies of the errata list are still available. The biography of Osler has not been translated, but the Press contemplates issuing an abridged one-volume edition.
Dedication. "To medical students in the hope that something of Osler's spirit may be conveyed to those of a generation that has not known him; and particularly to those in America, lest it be forgotten who it was that made it possible for them to work at the bedside in the wards."

7. The same—Special edition on India paper, bound in one volume, 1925, with pagination, illustrations, etc. as in No. 6.

⟦Of this 100 copies were printed in accordance with the usual practice of the Clarendon Press in the case of many of its larger works. These were printed in 1925 at the time of the first issue. They are bound in maroon-colored cloth; the ordinary two-volume edition was bound in a dark Oxford blue.

V. CLASSIFICATION OF GLIOMAS, 1926

8. A classification of the tumors of the glioma group on a histogenetic basis with a correlated study of prognosis. (With P. Bailey [1]) *Philadelphia, London & Montreal: J. B. Lippincott Co.,* 1926. 8vo, 4 p.l. [1st blank], 175 [1] pp. [108 halftone text figures; none inserted].

⟦This monograph is significant in the history of neurology since it represents the first serious attempt to classify gliomatous tumors of the central nervous system on a histological basis correlated with the life history of each type of growth. The analysis herein offered has become the basis of most subsequent classifications of tumors of the glioma group. The book, of which 1500 copies were issued, is still in print and has been only once translated (No. 9). A Russian edition was contemplated in 1931, but it evidently has not yet appeared. In a recent article Bailey relates the story of how this monograph came to be written (A review of modern conceptions of the structure and classification of tumors derived from the medullary epithelium. *J. belge Neurol. Psychiat.,* Oct. 1938, 38: 759–782).
Dedication. The book is appropriately dedicated "To Professor S. Ramón y Cajal and the distinguished disciples of his school of Spanish neurohistologists."

9. Die Gewebs-Verschiedenheit der Hirngliome und ihre Bedeutung für die Prognose. Nach einer Ergänzung der ersten englischen Ausgabe durch die Verfasser ins Deutsche übersetzt von Alfred Cammann, Pathol. Institut der Universität Göttingen. *Jena: Verlag von Gustav Fischer, 1930.* 8vo, x, 166 pp. [107 text figures].

⟨This translation is based upon a corrected and extended text and bibliography which is not yet available in English. The illustrations are for the most part from the same plates as in the English edition but are more successfully reproduced; a few substitutions have been made. There is also an added section on histological methods. It is bound in grey cloth with blue lettering. The "Geleitwort" is signed by Georg B. Gruber and is dated "Göttingen, 18.viii.29." The English edition was based upon a total of 412 verified tumors. In the authors' introduction to the German edition (pp. vii–ix) statistics are given based on 690 verified cases. New terms, such as "glioblastoma multiforme" (for "spongioblastoma multiforme"), have been adopted in the translation, and the "neuroblastomas" were dropped from the classification; there are other terminological changes in the text.

VI. STUDIES IN INTRACRANIAL PHYSIOLOGY, 1926

10. Studies in intracranial physiology and surgery. The third circulation. The hypophysis. The gliomas. *London: Humphrey Milford, Oxford University Press, 1926.* 8vo, xii, 146 pp. [16 text figures, none inserted].

⟨The Cameron Prize Lectures delivered at the University of Edinburgh October 19, 20, 22, 1925, and issued as one of the series of "Oxford Medical Publications." The lectures appeared in abridged form in the *Lancet* during October and November 1925 (see below Nos. 238, 239, 240). The first lecture is Dr. Cushing's most recent discussion of the physiology of the cerebrospinal fluid. The lectures have not been translated and are out of print at the Oxford University Press both in New York and London.
Dedication. "To my successive appointees in the 'Old Hunterian' at the Johns Hopkins Medical School and to the Arthur Tracy Cabot Fellows since 1912 in charge of the Laboratory of Surgical Research at Harvard [names listed] and also to the succession of my Assistant Residents both in Baltimore and Boston," etc. [names also listed].

11. The same. American edition with cancel title bearing imprint *New York: Oxford University Press 1926.* Pagination etc. as in No. 10.

VII. PATHOLOGICAL FINDINGS IN ACROMEGALY, 1927

12. The pathological findings in four autopsied cases of acromegaly with a discussion of their significance. (With L. M. Davidoff) *New York: Rockefeller Institute for Medical*

Research (Monograph No. 22), 1927. 8vo, 1 p.l., 131 pp. [104 halftone text figures].

⟦This monograph represents the most detailed pathological study of individual cases of acromegaly available in the literature. It supplements and expands that given in No. 1 above, and also that from Dr. Cushing's clinic by Dott and Bailey in 1925 (No. 237 below). The monograph was issued unbound in heavy blue cardboard covers, dated April 23, 1927. There is no dedication and the report has not been translated.

VIII. TUMORS ARISING FROM BLOOD-VESSELS, 1928

13. Tumors arising from the blood-vessels of the brain. Angiomatous malformations and hemangioblastomas. (With P. Bailey) *Springfield, Ill.: Charles C. Thomas*, 1928. 8vo, x, 219 [3] pp. [159 halftone text figures; none inserted].

⟦A beautifully illustrated monograph based on 29 cases of one of the rarest and most interesting groups of intracranial tumors; in Dr. Cushing's series they make up nearly two per cent of all intracranial tumors. It is the first of a series of four monographs by Dr. Cushing (Nos. 16, 20, 24) to be published by Mr. Charles C Thomas. One thousand copies were printed of which 270 bore the English imprint (No. 14). A few copies of the American edition are still in print. The book was enthusiastically reviewed, *e.g.* in the *Lancet* (June 15, 1929) and in the *British Medical Journal* (May 25, 1929). There is no dedication.

14. The same—with cancel title bearing imprint: *London: Baillière, Tindall and Cox*, 1928. Pagination etc. the same.

IX. CONSECRATIO MEDICI, 1928

15. Consecratio medici and other papers. *Boston: Little, Brown, and Company*, 1928. 8vo, 2 p.l., 276 pp.

⟦In this volume, which was issued in November 1928, are reprinted the following of Dr. Cushing's literary essays: Nos. 245, 72, 132, 157, 180, 198, 208, 213, 216, 221, 224, 234, 247, 260. The publishers printed 2000 copies in the original issue, and there were two uncorrected additional printings of 1000 and 1010 copies respectively, making a total of 4010. The book was out of print but has just been reissued (500 copies). There has been no English edition or foreign translation.

X. INTRACRANIAL TUMOURS, 1932

16. Intracranial tumours. Notes upon a series of two thousand verified cases with surgical-mortality percentages pertaining thereto. *Springfield, Ill.: Charles C Thomas*, 1932. 8vo, xii, 150 pp., 1 l. [111 halftone text figures].

⟦A monograph based upon a report made at the First International Neurological Congress at Bern, August 31, 1931. Dr. Cushing had commenced his postgraduate studies at Bern in 1900-01 and in returning thirty years later to make this report he spoke of the early days there under Hugo Kronecker and Theodor Kocher. His detailed statistics, based upon his life's study of intracranial tumors were then presented, and he concluded: "This report, which is certainly the last I shall ever attempt to make on the subject of brain tumours as a whole, cannot properly be concluded without paying tribute to my successive assistants and co-workers during these past many years who have faced the brunt of the work and shared the responsibilities." The edition, which was published in this country on March 10, 1932, consisted of 2039 copies, of which 180 bore the English imprint. The book is still in print. *Dedication.* "In affection and gratitude to my successive co-workers and assistants in neurosurgery."

17. The same—with cancel title bearing imprint, *London: Baillière, Tindall and Cox,* 1932. Pagination etc. the same.

18. Intrakranielle Tumoren. Bericht über 2000 bestätigte Fälle mit der zugehörigen Mortalitätsstatistik. Mit Ergänzungen des Verfassers übersetzt und herausgegeben von F. K. Kessel, Berlin. *Berlin: Verlag von Julius Springer,* 1935. 8vo, viii, 139 [1] pp. [111 halftone text figures].

⟮The German edition was issued without change of text except for: (i) an occasional explanatory footnote; (ii) bracketed statements bringing the end results of the cited cases up to date; (iii) a brief note concerning basophilic adenomas of the pituitary body; and (iv) an appendix in which an abstract was given of the end-result study made by W. P. Van Wagenen (see No. 627). The two-page "Vorwort" by Dr. Cushing is dated "New Haven, 9 Januar 1935." The figures are excellently reproduced, as in No. 16. The dedication is omitted.

19. Tumeurs intracraniennes. Étude analytique de 2000 tumeurs vérifiées et de leur mortalité opératoire. Édition revue et augmentée par l'auteur et comprenant deux études sur les résultats éloignés du traitement opératoire des tumeurs intracraniennes par W. P. Van Wagenen (Rochester, New York) et Hugh Cairns (Londres). Traduction française de Jean Rossier (Lausanne). *Paris: Masson et Cie., Éditeurs,* 1937. 8vo, 3 p.l., 194 [1] pp. [111 halftone text figures].

⟮The French translation is also based upon a corrected and extended text and it has appended the special reports of end results by W. P. Van Wagenen and H. W. B. Cairns (see below Nos. 627 and 322). Dr. Cushing contributed a special preface dated "New Haven, le 14 décembre 1936." Unbound copies broché were issued in a bright yellow cover which, save for the abbreviated imprint, substantially duplicates the title. The French edition is still in print.

XI. PITUITARY BODY AND HYPOTHALAMUS, 1932

20. Papers relating to the pituitary body, hypothalamus and parasympathetic nervous system. *Springfield, Ill.: Charles C Thomas,* 1932. 8vo, vii, 234 pp. [99 text figures, 97 in halftone, and 2 in color (figs. 25 and 83)].

¶This volume contains Dr. Cushing's four principal contributions on pituitary-hypothalamic interrelationships: (i) the first is his Lister Memorial Lecture, "Neurohypophysial mechanisms from a clinical standpoint," delivered July 9, 1930, in which the problem of nervous control of the posterior lobe of the pituitary is discussed in detail with particular references to the neuro-endocrine mechanisms involved in diabetes insipidus, adiposity, heat regulation, pathological sleep and carbohydrate metabolism; the clinical and physiological manifestations of these conditions are also described. The lecture as originally published in the *Lancet* (see below No. 287) was abbreviated and illustrations were omitted. The present reprint contains the full text with 24 halftone illustrations.

¶(ii) The second section contains the series of eight notes originally published in the *Proceedings of the National Academy of Sciences* (see below Nos. 294 and 302) which appeared under the general title "Posterior pituitary hormones and the parasympathetic nervous system." The first six papers formed the basis of the William Henry Welch Lecture at Mount Sinai Hospital in New York, April 30, 1931. They contain a detailed account of Dr. Cushing's well known observations on the effects of intraventricular injections in man of pilocarpine and pituitrin and include also a full statement of his evidence for the existence of a parasympathetic center in the hypothalamic area.

¶(iii) The third section is a reprinting without additions of Dr. Cushing's original description of the syndrome of pituitary basophilism which is now widely referred to as "the Cushing syndrome" (see No. 298 below). It also includes the *Addendum* on pituitary basophilism reprinted from No. 303 below.

¶(iv) The fourth section, "Peptic ulcer and the interbrain" is reprinted from No. 301 below, being the basis of the fourth Balfour Lecture given April 8, 1931, at the University of Toronto. It contains a colored illustration showing haemorrhagic erosions and perforation of the stomach, and a full statement of Dr. Cushing's concept of the relation of the hypothalamus to gastric disturbances. An edition of 1775 copies was issued, 156 of which bore the English imprint; it is still in print. There is no dedication.

21. The same—with cancel title bearing imprint, *London: Baillière, Tindall and Cox*, 1932. Pagination etc. unchanged.

XII. FROM A SURGEON'S JOURNAL, 1936

22. From a surgeon's journal 1915–1918. *Boston: Little, Brown, and Company*, 1936. 8vo, frontispiece, xxi, 534 pp., 34 inserted halftone illustrations [miscellaneous, unnumbered text figures].

¶This book is made up of extracts from Dr. Cushing's voluminous War Diary, only very brief portions of which have previously been published (see Nos. 157 and 317). The size of the various printings was as follows: 1st, 7500; 2nd, 2500; 3rd, 1000; 4th, 1960; 5th, 2000; 1500 in addition went to Messrs. Constable for the English and Canadian edition. A total of 17,460 has been printed to date. The book is still in print. The volume covers the period from March 1915, when Dr. Cushing first went to Europe to the *Ambulance Américaine* with a Harvard Unit, until November 14, 1918. The author was eventually discharged at Washington,

D. C., April 9, 1919. The book is illustrated with Dr. Cushing's photographs, maps and pencil sketches of contemporary events.
Dedication. "To K. C. for her sympathy and understanding through all this."

23. The same—with cancel title bearing imprint, *London: Constable & Co., Ltd.*, 1936. The pagination etc. are the same.

⟨This issue is identical with the American edition save for the cancel pp. (373–4) where "Burberry raincoat" has been changed to "waterproof raincoat."

XIII. MENINGIOMAS, 1938

24. Meningiomas. Their classification, regional behaviour, life history, and surgical end results. (With L. Eisenhardt). *Springfield, Ill.: Charles C Thomas,* 1938. Large 8vo, xiv, 785 pp. [with 685 text figures; figs. 504 and 540 in color].

⟨The present treatise was commenced in 1915 soon after the completion of his volume on the pituitary disorders, and it therefore represents nearly twenty-five years of work; by common consent it is regarded as Dr. Cushing's greatest clinical monograph. It is the embodiment of all the things he has stood for during his career as a clinician: his painstaking case records and photographs, his unusual artistic ability evident in his own numerous operative sketches, and his extraordinary knowledge of the day-to-day life of his patients. To quote a reviewer in a recent number of the *Journal of the American Medical Association* (Jan. 12, 1939, p. 175): "If the art falls into disrepute because of present practices it will be from neglect of the main lesson which he [H. C.] attempted to teach."

⟨In the "Foreword" (dated "New Haven, Connecticut, December 1937") it is stated that the monograph on acoustic tumors (No. 3) was an outgrowth of the present work, since the VIIIth nerve tumors were thought at first to be of meningeal origin. The book is printed by Charles Thomas, who had the materials set up by the George Banta Publishing Company in a type called Century Schoolbook. The title page was designed by Mr. Carl Purington Rollins, printer to Yale University. It has the advantage of giving a very legible five-inch type page which heeds all aesthetic consideration of typography; 1765 copies were printed, none with English imprint. A German translation is being made by F. K. Kessel for Julius Springer which will probably appear in 1940.
Dedication. "To our co-workers and the patients who have contributed to this record."

XIV. THE MEDICAL CAREER, 1940

24a. The medical career and other papers. *Boston: Little, Brown, and Company,* 1940. 8vo, viii, 302 pp.

⟨This volume, which was in press at the time of Dr. Cushing's death and which appeared in February 1940, contains the following essays and biographical sketches: Nos. 274, 295, 309, 319, 316, 279, 318, 281, 315, 320, 206, 253, 296, 326, 47, 310, 330a. There were 2000 copies printed and issued simultaneously with a reprinting of the *Consecratio medici* (see No. 15).

III. ADDRESSES, PAPERS IN JOURNALS AND REPORTS

ADDRESSES, PAPERS IN JOURNALS AND REPORTS

Abbreviations of journal titles are given in accordance with World List (*2nd ed., 1934*) *conventions.*

1898

25. Typhoidal cholecystitis and cholelithiasis. Report of a case without previous history of typhoid fever, and discussion of a possible agglutinative reaction in the bile and its relation to stone formation. *Johns Hopk. Hosp. Bull.*, May 1898, 9: 91–95.

26. Haematomyelia from gunshot wounds of the spine. A report of two cases, with recovery following symptoms of hemilesion of the cord. *Amer. J. med. Sci.*, June 1898, 115: 654–683.

⟨Preliminary report presented before the Johns Hopkins Hospital Medical Society, May 3, 1897. See *Johns Hopk. Hosp. Bull.*, Aug.–Sept. 1897, 8: 195–196.

27. Operative wounds of the thoracic duct. Report of a case with suture of the duct. *Ann. Surg.*, June 1898, 27: 719–728.

⟨Read before the Johns Hopkins Medical Society, March 20, 1898.

28. Cocaine anaesthesia in the treatment of certain cases of hernia and in operations for thyroid tumors. *Johns Hopk. Hosp. Bull.*, Aug. 1898, 9: 192–193.

⟨Remarks upon cases exhibited at the Johns Hopkins Hospital Medical Society, May 8, 1898.

29. Laparotomy for intestinal perforation in typhoid fever. A report of four cases, with a discussion of the diagnostic signs of perforation. *Johns Hopk. Hosp. Bull.*, Nov. 1898, 9: 257–269.

30. Discussion of: Two cases of pylorectomy. By Dr. Finney. *Johns Hopk. Hosp. Bull.*, Dec. 1898, 9: 295–296.

1899

31. Acute diffuse gonococcus peritonitis. *Johns Hopk. Hosp. Bull.*, May 1899, 10: 75–81.

32. Remarks upon a case of jejunal fistula. *Johns Hopk. Hosp. Bull.*, July 1899, 10: 136–137.

⟨Presented before the Johns Hopkins Hospital Medical Society, March 6, 1899. See also abstract: *Maryland med. J.*, 1899, 41: 140.

33. Observations upon the origin of gall-bladder infections

and upon the experimental formation of gall-stones. *Johns Hopk. Hosp. Bull.,* Aug.–Sept. 1899, 10: 166–170.

¶Remarks before the Johns Hopkins Hospital Medical Society to accompany Dr. Hunner's report of a case of typhoidal cholecystitis.

34. Splenectomy for primary splenic anemia. *Maryland med. J.,* 1899, 41: 140. See also No. 184.

1900

35. The employment of local anaesthesia in the radical cure of certain cases of hernia, with a note upon the nervous anatomy of the inguinal region. *Ann. Surg.,* Jan. 1900, 31: 1–34.

¶Brief report in: *Maryland med. J.,* 1899, 41: 140.

36. Observations upon the neural anatomy of the inguinal region relative to the performance of herniotomy under local anaesthesia. *Johns Hopk. Hosp. Bull.,* March 1900, 11: 58–64.

37. Exploratory laparotomy under local anesthesia for acute abdominal symptoms occurring in the course of typhoid fever. *Philad. med. J.* [Special typhoid fever number] March 1900, 5: 501–508.

38. A method of total extirpation of the Gasserian ganglion for trigeminal neuralgia. By a route through the temporal fossa and beneath the middle meningeal artery. *J. Amer. med. Ass.,* April 28, 1900, 34: 1035–1041.

¶Presented at a meeting of the College of Physicians of Philadelphia, April 20, 1900.

39. Laparotomy for intestinal perforation in typhoid fever. A report of four cases occurring in 1898. *Johns Hopk. Hosp. Rep.,* 1900, 8: 209–240.

40. Experimental and surgical notes upon the bacteriology of the upper portion of the alimentary canal, with observations on the establishment there of an amicrobic state as a preliminary to operative procedures on the stomach and small intestine. (With L. E. Livingood) *Johns Hopk. Hosp. Rep.,* 1900, 9: 543–591.

¶In: Contributions to the science of medicine dedicated by his pupils to William Henry Welch on the 25th anniversary of his doctorate. *Baltimore: Johns Hopkins Press,* 1900. 4to, vii, 1066 pp.

41. A comparative study of some members of a pathogenic group of bacilli of the hog cholera or bac. enteritidis (Gärt-

ner) type, intermediate between the typhoid and colon groups. With the report of a case resembling typhoid fever, in which there occurred a post-febrile osteomyelitis due to such an intermediate bacillus. *Johns Hopk. Hosp. Bull.*, July–Aug. 1900, 11: 156–170.

42. Thrombosis of carotid artery. *Johns Hopk. Hosp. Bull.*, Oct. 1900, 11: 260.

ℂPresented before the Johns Hopkins Hospital Medical Society, June 18, 1900.

1901

43. Sur la laparotomie exploratrice précoce dans la perforation intestinale au cours de la fièvre typhoide. *Arch. gén. Méd.*, Jan. 1901, 187 (n.s. 5): 14–26.

ℂ"Traduit de l'américain par P. Lecène, interne des hôpitaux de Paris."

44. Concerning prompt surgical intervention for intestinal perforation in typhoid fever, with the relation of a case. *Ann. Surg.*, May 1901, 33: 544–557.

45. Concerning a definite regulatory mechanism of the vasomotor centre which controls blood pressure during cerebral compression. *Johns Hopk. Hosp. Bull.*, Sept. 1901, 12: 290–292.

46. Concerning the poisonous effect of pure sodium chloride solutions upon the nerve-muscle preparation. *Amer. J. Physiol.*, Oct. 1, 1901, 6: 77–90.

47. Haller and his native town. Letter from a post-graduate student. *Amer. Med.*, Oct. 5, 12, 1901, 2: 542–544; 580–582. (In No. 24a)

48. Differenze dell' irritabilità dei nervi e dei muscoli. *R.C. Accad. Lincei*, 1901, 10: 145–146.

ℂPublished also in French under the title: Différences entre l'irritabilité des nerfs et celle des muscles. *Arch. ital. Biol.*, 1902, 37: 63–64.

1902

49. Saline irrigations and infusions. In: S. S. Cohen's *System of physiologic therapeutics*. Philadelphia: P. Blakiston's Son & Co., 1902, 9: 279–296.

50. Physiologische und anatomische Beobachtungen über den Einfluss von Hirnkompression auf den intracraniellen

Kreislauf und über einige hiermit verwandte Erscheinungen. *Mitt. Grenzgeb. Med. Chir.,* 1902, 9: 773–808.

❡ "Aus der chirurgischen Klinik von Prof. Kocher in Bern." This paper was used as the experimental basis for Dr. Cushing's Mütter Lecture (see No. 52). Kocher in 1901 quoted in detail from the original manuscript, reproducing several illustrations, including three in color from experiment 26, p. 97 (Hirnerschütterung, Hirndruck und chirurgische Eingriffe bei Hirnkrankheiten. In: *Specielle Pathologie und Therapie.* Dr. Hermann Nothnagel, Ed. Wien: Alfred Hölder, 1901, 9: part III, 457 pp.).

51. On the avoidance of shock in major amputations by cocainization of large nerve-trunks preliminary to their division. With observations on blood-pressure changes in surgical cases. *Ann. Surg.,* Sept. 1902, 36: 321–345.

❡ Basis of the address in surgery before the Wisconsin State Medical Society, June 4, 1902. Also read before the Maryland Medical and Chirurgical Faculty, April 24, 1902. See *Trans. med. chir. Fac. Md.,* 1902, p. 17.

52. Some experimental and clinical observations concerning states of increased intracranial tension. *Amer. J. med. Sci.,* Sept. 1902, 124: 375–400.

❡ The Mütter Lecture [Philadelphia] for 1901. This contains the first reference to blood-pressure determinations (see No. 55).

53. Exhibition of surgical cases. A ninth case of Gasserian ganglion extirpation. *Johns Hopk. Hosp. Bull.,* Oct. 1902, 13: 248–249.

❡ Presented before the Johns Hopkins Hospital Medical Society, March 3, 1902.

54. Treatment by the tourniquet to counteract the vasomotor spasm of Raynaud's disease. *J. nerv. ment. Dis.,* Nov. 1902, 29: 657–663.

1903

55. On routine determinations of arterial tension in operating room and clinic. *Boston med. surg. J.,* March 5, 1903, 148: 250–256.

❡ Read at the Boston Medical Library, January 19, 1903. This paper marks the beginning of blood-pressure determinations in this country. Dr. Cushing had brought the Riva-Rocci instrument from Italy in 1901 and began at once to use it routinely in his surgical cases. He herein relates: "Two years ago, while on a tour among the Italian university towns, I had the good fortune in Pavia to be shown through the medical wards of the old Ospidale di S. Matteo by Dr. Orlandi, a colleague of Riva-Rocci, and to my great interest found that a simple 'home-made' adaptation of the latter's blood-pressure apparatus was in routine daily use at the bedside of every patient. . . . Thanks to Dr. Orlandi, I was given a model of the inflatable armlet which they employed, and practically the same form of apparatus . . . has been utilized at the Johns Hopkins Hospital with increasing satisfaction ever since." This paper led to the following report on blood-pressure determinations: *The division of surgery of the Medical School of Harvard University. Report of research work,* 1903–04. Dr. Cushing first mentioned the subject in September 1902 (see No. 52). Preliminary reports were also made before the Johns Hopkins Hospital Medical Society, November 17, 1902, by J. B. Briggs and H. W. Cook (see Nos. 397, 410).

56. The taste fibres and their independence of the N. trigeminus. Deductions from thirteen cases of Gasserian ganglion extirpation. *Johns Hopk. Hosp. Bull.,* March–April, 1903, 14: 71–78.

⟪Presented at the meeting of the American Physiological Society, held in Washington, December 31, 1902.

57. The surgical treatment of facial paralysis by nerve anastomosis. With the report of a successful case. *Ann. Surg.,* May 1903, 37: 641–659.

⟪Read before the Philadelphia Neurological Society, February 24, 1903. Brief report: *J. nerv. ment. Dis.,* 1903, 30: 367–368, under the title, A case of traumatic facial paralysis treated by nerve anastomosis. A preliminary report.

58. The blood-pressure reaction of acute cerebral compression, illustrated by cases of intracranial hemorrhage. *Amer. J. med. Sci.,* June 1903, n.s.125, 1017–1044.

⟪A sequel to the Mütter Lecture for 1901.

59. Exhibition of two cases of radicular paralysis of the brachial plexus. One from the pressure of a cervical rib, with operation. The other of uncertain origin. (With H. M. Thomas [1]) *Johns Hopk. Hosp. Bull.,* Nov. 1903, 14: 315–319.

1904

60. Perineal zoster, with notes upon cutaneous segmentation post-axial to the lower limb. *Amer. J. med. Sci.,* March 1904, n.s.127, 375–391.

⟪Read before the Johns Hopkins Hospital Medical Society, December 7, 1903. See *Johns Hopk. Hosp. Bull.,* May 1904, 15: 172.

61. Pneumatic tourniquets: with especial reference to their use in craniotomies. *Med. News, N.Y.,* March 26, 1904, 84: 577–580.

62. Intradural tumor of the cervical meninges. With early restoration of function in the cord after removal of the tumor. *Ann. Surg.,* June 1904, 39: 934–955.

63. The sensory distribution of the fifth cranial nerve. *Johns Hopk. Hosp. Bull.*, July–August 1904, 15: 213–232.

1905

64. The special field of neurological surgery. *Cleveland med. J.*, Jan. 1905, 4: 1–25. Also: *Johns Hopk. Hosp. Bull.*, March 1905, 16: 77–87.

⟦An address delivered before the Academy of Medicine of Cleveland, November 18, 1904.

65. The surgical aspects of major neuralgia of the trigeminal nerve. A report of twenty cases of operation on the Gasserian ganglion, with anatomic and physiologic notes on the consequences of its removal. *J. Amer. med. Ass.*, March 11, 18, 25, April 1, 8, 1905, 44: 773–778; 860–865; 920–929; 1002–1008; 1088–1093.

⟦Presented at a meeting of the Montreal Medico-Chirurgical Society, February 5, 1904.

66. Diseases of the nervous system. In: Osler's *Principles and practice of medicine,* 6th ed. New York and London: D. Appleton and Co., 1905, pp. 867–1110.

⟦In the preface, Osler offers thanks "to H. M. Thomas of the Neurological Department, and to Harvey Cushing of the Surgical Clinic, who have revised the section on the Nervous System."

67. Introduction [179–180] to: Comparative surgery; with illustrative cases. By C. M. Faris, H. C. Thacher, J. F. Ortschild, and F. C. Beall. *Johns Hopk. Hosp. Bull.*, May 1905, 16: 179–199.

⟦Presented before Johns Hopkins Hospital Medical Society, April 17, 1905. *Johns Hopk. Hosp. Bull.*, June 1905, 16: 238–239.

68. Concerning surgical intervention for the intracranial hemorrhages of the new-born. *Amer. J. med. Sci.*, Oct. 1905, n.s. 130: 563–581.

⟦Presented at the Philadelphia meeting of the American Neurological Association, June 2, 1905.

69. The establishment of cerebral hernia as a decompressive measure for inaccessible brain tumors; with the description of intermuscular methods of making the bone defect in temporal and occipital regions. *Surg. Gynec. Obstet.*, Oct. 1905, 1: 297–314.

70. Arteriovenous aneurysm of the occipital vessels. *N.Y. med. J.*, Dec. 23, 1905, 82: 1305–1310.

1906

71. On preservation of the nerve supply to the brow, in the operative approach to the Gasserian ganglion. *Ann. Surg.,* Jan. 1906, 43: 1–4.

72. Dr. Garth: the Kit-Kat Poet (1661–1718). *Johns Hopk. Hosp. Bull.,* Jan. 1906, 17: 1–17.

⟨Read at a meeting of the Johns Hopkins Hospital Historical Club, December 12, 1904. In No. 15.

73. Exhibition of surgical cases. Case I. Ruptured brachial plexus. Case II. von Recklinghausen's disease. (With Mr. Langnecker and Mr. Helmholz) *Johns Hopk. Hosp. Bull.,* March 1906, 17: 93–94.

⟨Presented before Johns Hopkins Hospital Medical Society, December 18, 1905.

74. Instruction in operative medicine. With the description of a course given in the Hunterian Laboratory of Experimental Medicine. *Johns Hopk. Hosp. Bull.,* May 1906, 17: 123–134. Also: *Yale med. J.,* April 1906, 12: 855–879.

⟨An address before the Yale Medical Alumni Association at New Haven, February 23, 1906.

75. The holders of the gold-headed cane as book collectors. *Johns Hopk. Hosp. Bull.,* May 1906, 17: 166–169.

⟨Presented at the symposium on the gold-headed cane, Johns Hopkins Historical Club, January 29, 1906.

76. Cases of spontaneous intracranial hemorrhage associated with trigeminal nevi. *J. Amer. med. Ass.,* July 21, 1906, 47: 178–183.

⟨Read in the Section on Surgery and Anatomy of the American Medical Association, at the 57th annual session, June 1906.

77. Elephantiasis nervorum of the scalp: a manifestation of von Recklinghausen's disease. (With H. F. Helmholz [1]) *Amer. J. med. Sci.,* Sept. 1906, n.s. 132: 355–378.

78. Sexual infantilism with optic atrophy in cases of tumor affecting the hypophysis cerebri. *J. nerv. ment. Dis.,* Nov. 1906, 33: 704–716.

⟨Read at the meeting of the American Neurological Association, June 4–5, 1906. Referring to this paper, Dr. Cushing in a footnote to his second Harvey Lecture (see No. 307), states: "In December, 1902, there died in Dr. Osler's wards at the Johns Hopkins Hospital a sexually undeveloped girl of 16 with the symptoms described by Babinski, whose case was subsequently reported in my first paper which in any way pertained to the pituitary body."

79. Introduction (with P. K. Gilman) [369–370] to: Comparative surgery. Second series of reports. By F. W. Bancroft and E. S. Cross; G. R. Henry; W. D. Gatch; J. G. Hopkins; A. R. Dochez; W. Von Gerber; and G. J. Heuer. *Johns Hopk. Hosp. Bull.,* Dec. 1906, 17: 369–393.

1907

80. A discussion of some immediate and some remote consequences of cranial injuries, based on three clinical histories which illustrate the extradural, subcortical, and intermeningeal types of intracranial haemorrhages. *N.Y. med. J.,* Jan. 19, 26, Feb. 2, 1907, 85: 97–107; 161–169; 208–216.
⟪The Wesley M. Carpenter Lecture delivered at the New York Academy of Medicine, October 18, 1906.

81. Exhibition of cases. Decompressive craniectomy for brain tumor; Gasserian ganglion operation for major neuralgia; exploratory craniotomy for Jacksonian epilepsy originating in the motor area of the lower extremity. *Johns Hopk. Hosp. Bull.,* April 1907, 18: 142–145.
⟪Meeting of the Johns Hopkins Hospital Medical Society, December 3, 1906.

82. Remarks on some further modifications in the Gasserian ganglion operation for trigeminal neuralgia (sensory-root evulsion). *Trans. Sth. surg. gynec. Ass., Nashville, Tenn.,* 1907, 19: 480–485.

83. Remarks on the surgical treatment of facial paralysis and of trigeminal neuralgia, with exhibition of patients. *Trans. Amer. surg. Ass.,* 1907, 25: 275–280; discussion: 281–283.

84. Introduction (with J. F. Ortschild) [459–462] to: Comparative surgery. Third series of reports. By J. T. Geraghty; J. W. Churchman; S. J. Crowe; F. F. Gundrum; C. W. Mills; R. D. McClure and H. F. Derge; C. H. Bryant; H. M. Evans and A. G. Brenizer. *Johns Hopk. Hosp. Bull.,* Dec. 1907, 18: 459–480.
⟪In the paper by Evans and Brenizer (see No. 432) is a footnote signed "H.C." in which are described personal observations on peculiar changes in disposition of the operated animals, probably due to disordered nutrition and resembling the effects of direct removal of frontal lobes.

1908

85. Presentation of cases. The subtemporal decompressive operation for the relief of pressure symptoms due to fracture

of base of skull. *Johns Hopk. Hosp. Bull.*, Feb. 1908, 19: 48–49.

⟦Read before the Johns Hopkins Hospital Medical Society, October 7, 1907.

86. Experimental and clinical notes on chronic valvular lesions in the dog and their possible relation to a future surgery of the cardiac valves. [With J. R. B. Branch] *J. med. Res.*, Feb. 1908, n.s. 12: 471–486.

87. Technical methods of performing certain cranial operations. *Interst. med. J.*, 1908, 15: 171–187.

⟦Extracts from an address before the St. Louis Surgical Society, December 16, 1907.

88. Technical methods of performing certain cranial operations. *Surg. Gynec. Obstet.*, March 1908, 6: 227–246.

⟦Read before the St. Louis Surgical Society December 16, 1907. Certain paragraphs in this article are in amplification of the views expressed in a chapter in Keen's *System of surgery*, Vol. III (see No. 93).

89. Removal of a subcortical cystic tumor at a second-stage operation without anesthesia. (With H. M. Thomas [1]) *J. Amer. med. Ass.*, March 14, 1908, 50: 847–856.

⟦Read in the Section on Nervous and Mental Diseases of the American Medical Association at the 58th annual session, held at Atlantic City, June, 1907.

90. Subtemporal decompressive operations for the intracranial complications associated with bursting fractures of the skull. *Ann. Surg.*, May 1908, 47: 641–644. Also: *Trans. Sth. surg. gynec. Ass., Nashville, Tenn.*, 1908, 20: 324–330.

⟦Read before the Southern Surgical and Gynecological Association, New Orleans, December 1907.

91. Obstructive hydrocephalus following cerebrospinal meningitis, with intraventricular injection of antimeningitis serum (Flexner). (With F. J. Sladen) *J. exp. Med.*, July 1908, 10: 548–556.

92. Subtemporal decompression in a case of chronic nephritis with uremia; with especial consideration of the neuroretinal lesion. (With J. Bordley, Jr.) *Amer. J. med. Sci.*, Oct. 1908, n.s. 136: 484–504.

93. Surgery of the head. In: *Surgery, its principles and practice.* W. W. Keen, Ed. Philadelphia: W. B. Saunders Co., 1908, 3: 17–276.

⟨This is Dr. Cushing's first systematic treatise on the technique of neurological surgery. The paper was widely quoted, and during the World War was reprinted by the U. S. Surgeon-General in an Army handbook for traumatic surgery of the head. See Nos. 166, 175.

1909

94. Cases of brain tumor. *Johns Hopk. Hosp. Bull.*, Jan. 1909, 20: 22.

⟨Presented before the Johns Hopkins Hospital Medical Society, November 2, 1908.

95. Some principles of cerebral surgery. *J. Amer. med. Ass.*, Jan. 16, 1909, 52: 184–192.

⟨Read in the joint meeting of the Section on Surgery and Anatomy and the Section on Laryngology and Otology of the American Medical Association, at the 59th annual session at Chicago, June 1908.

96. Observations on choked disc, with especial reference to decompressive cranial operations. (With J. Bordley, Jr. [1]) *J. Amer. med. Ass.*, Jan. 30, 1909, 52: 353–360.

⟨Read in the joint meeting of the Section on Nervous and Mental Diseases, and the Section on Ophthalmology of the American Medical Association, at the 59th annual session at Chicago, June 1908.

97. Observations on experimentally induced choked disc. (With J. Bordley, Jr.) *Johns Hopk. Hosp. Bull.*, April 1909, 20: 95–101.

98. Is the pituitary gland essential to the maintenance of life? (With L. L. Reford [1]) *Johns Hopk. Hosp. Bull.*, April 1909, 20: 105–107.

⟨Read before the American Physiological Society, Baltimore, December 30, 1908. Preliminary note in: *Amer. J. Physiol.*, 1908–09, 23: xxvii–xxviii.

99. A note upon the faradic stimulation of the postcentral gyrus in conscious patients. *Brain*, May 1909, 32: 44–53.

⟨Presented at a meeting of the American Physiological Society, December 30, 1908. Preliminary note in: *Amer. J. Physiol.*, 1908–09, 23: xxvi. The observations recorded in this paper established the sensory function of the parietal lobes in human subjects.

100. Discussion of: Prophylactic use of hexamethylenamin in cerebrospinal meningitis. By S. J. Crowe. *Johns Hopk. Hosp. Bull.*, May 1909, 20: 154.

⟨Meeting of the Johns Hopkins Hospital Medical Society, February 1, 1909.

101. Report of the Committee on the Osler Testimonial. *Bull. med. chir. Fac. Md.*, June 1909, 1: 238–240.

102. Some aspects of the pathological physiology of intracranial tumors. *Boston med. surg. J.*, July 15, 1909, 161: 71–80.

❡A lecture under the auspices of the Cancer Commission of Harvard University, February 25, 1909. This paper in substance was given also before the New York Neurological Society at the Academy of Medicine, April 6, 1909; the Chicago Medical Society, Oct. 27, 1909; the Associated Physicians of Long Island, Jan. 29, 1910; and the American Neurological Association in Washington, June 1911.

103. A method of combining exploration and decompression for cerebral tumors which prove to be inoperable. *Trans. Amer. surg. Ass.*, 1909, 27: 565–572. Also: *Surg. Gynec. Obstet.*, July 1909, 9: 1–5.

104. The hypophysis cerebri. Clinical aspects of hyperpituitarism and of hypopituitarism. *J. Amer. med. Ass.*, July 24, 1909, 53: 249–255.

❡The Oration on Surgery, read in the Section on Surgery of the American Medical Association, at the 60th annual session, held at Atlantic City, June 1909.

105. Cases of cerebellar tumor, with the statistics of thirty operations. *Interst. med. J.*, Sept. 1909, 16: 607–613.

❡Remarks upon cases exhibited before the Johns Hopkins Hospital Medical Society, May 3, 1909. Report of meeting: *Johns Hopk. Hosp. Bull.*, Sept. 1909, 20: 291.

106. Alterations in the color fields in cases of brain tumor. (With J. Bordley, Jr. [1]) *Arch. Ophthal., N.Y.*, Sept. 1909, 38: 451–462.

❡Presented [by H.C.] at a meeting of the American Neurological Association, New York, May 27, 1909. For discussion see: Inversion and interlacing of the color fields, an early symptom of brain tumor. *J. Amer. Med. Ass.*, 1909, 53: 316; *J. nerv. ment. Dis.*, 1909, 36: 549–553; *Trans. Amer. neurol. Ass.*, 1910, 69–72.

107. Effects of hypophyseal transplantation following total hypophysectomy in the canine. (With S. J. Crowe [1] and J. Homans [3]) *Quart. J. exp. Physiol.*, Oct. 1909, 2: 389–400.

108. Partial hypophysectomy for acromegaly with remarks on the function of the hypophysis. *Ann. Surg.*, Dec. 1909, 50: 1002–1017.

❡Presented at the XVIth International Medical Congress at Budapest, September 1909.

1910

109. Recent observations on tumours of the brain and their surgical treatment. *Lancet,* Jan. 8, 1910, 1: 90–94.

¶[Abstract of the fourth William Mitchell Banks Memorial Lecture, delivered at the University of Liverpool, August 4, 1909.

110. The functions of the pituitary body. *Amer. J. med. Sci.,* April 1910, n.s. 139: 473–484.

¶[Read at the combined session of the American Physiological Society and Section K of the American Association for the Advancement of Science, Boston, December 28, 1909.

111. Experimental hypophysectomy. (With S. J. Crowe [1] and J. Homans [3]) *Johns Hopk. Hosp. Bull.,* May 1910, 21: 127–169.

112. Strangulation of the nervi abducentes by lateral branches of the basilar artery in cases of brain tumour. With an explanation of some obscure palsies on the basis of arterial constriction. *Brain,* Oct. 1910, 33: 204–235.

¶[Presented at a meeting of the American Neurological Association, Washington, May 2, 1910.

113. Concerning the secretion of the infundibular lobe of the pituitary body and its presence in the cerebrospinal fluid. (With E. Goetsch) *Amer. J. Physiol.,* Nov. 1, 1910, 27: 60–86.

¶[Presented before the American Association of Pathologists and Bacteriologists, Washington, June 1910.

114. The special field of neurological surgery: five years later. *Johns Hopk. Hosp. Bull.,* Nov. 1910, 21: 325–339. Also: *Cleveland med. J.,* Nov. 1910, 9: 827–863.

¶[An address, fragments of which were presented before the alumni of the Lakeside Hospital, in Cleveland, January 1910, the Cleveland Academy of Medicine, October 21, 1910, and the Syracuse Medical Alumni Association, Syracuse, June 6, 1910.

115. Tumors of the brain and meninges. In: *Osler's Modern medicine.* Philadelphia: Lea & Febiger, 1910, 7: 418–458. British edition: *A system of medicine* (Osler and McCrae). London: Henry Frowde, 1910, 7: 418–458.

116. Hydrocephalus. In: *Osler's Modern medicine.* Philadelphia: Lea & Febiger, 1910, 7: 459–466. British edition: *A system of medicine* (Osler and McCrae). London: Henry Frowde, 1910, 7: 459–466.

117. Letter [pp. 16–18] in: *Western Reserve University. The Medical Department. Endowment Fund.* [Cleveland, 1910] 4to, 18 pp.

¶In appendix [pp. 11–18] containing "Letters from distinguished medical teachers and educators."

1911

118. Brain tumors and their surgical treatment. *Can. Lancet,* March 1911, 44: 507–509.

¶Abstract of address at the Academy of Medicine, Toronto, February 7, 1911.

119. Carbohydrate tolerance and the posterior lobe of the hypophysis cerebri. An experimental and clinical study. (With E. Goetsch [1] and C. Jacobson [3]) *Johns Hopk. Hosp. Bull.,* June 1911, 22: 165–190.

¶Presented [by H.C.] at the meeting of the American Physiological Society, held in New Haven, December 1910.

120. Distortions of the visual fields in cases of brain tumor. Statistical studies. (First paper) (With G. J. Heuer) *Johns Hopk. Hosp. Bull.,* June 1911, 22: 190–195.

¶This communication is the first of a series of five papers, the four to follow dealing respectively with dyschromatopsia and with the binasal, bitemporal and homonymous hemianopsias which have been observed in a series of 200 cases of brain tumor. [The series eventually included seven papers: See also Nos. 122, 124, 146, 167, 201, 514.]

121. The control of bleeding in operations for brain tumors. With the description of silver "clips" for the occlusion of vessels inaccessible to the ligature. *Ann. Surg.,* July 1911, 54: 1–19. Also: *Trans. Amer. surg. Ass.,* 1911, 29: 389–410.

¶Read by title before the American Surgical Association, June 1911. This paper introduced the use of silver clips in neurosurgery.

122. Distortions of the visual fields in cases of brain tumor. (Second paper) Dyschromatopsia in relation to stages of choked disk. (With G. J. Heuer) *J. Amer. med. Ass.,* July 15, 1911, 57: 200–208. [Abstract of discussion, pp. 219–220.]

¶Read in the Section on Ophthalmology of the American Medical Association at the 62nd annual session held at Los Angeles, June 1911.

123. Dyspituitarism. *Harvey Lect.,* 1910–1911, 31–45.

¶Editor's footnote: "This lecture, of December 10, 1910, owing to its extensive case reports and copious illustrations, does not lend itself in its original forms to publication in this series. The author has incorporated much new material since the lecture was delivered, and the J. B. Lippincott Company will publish it in full as a separate monograph. The accompanying text is an excerpt and gives the clinical subdivisions in accordance with which the author has provisionally grouped his numerous illustrations of hypophyseal disease." [See No. 1.]

1912

124. Distortions of the visual fields in cases of brain tumor. (Third paper) Binasal hemianopsia. (With C. B. Walker) *Arch. Ophthal., N.Y.,* Nov. 1912, 41: 559–598.

The pituitary body and its disorders. See Nos. 1, 2.

1913

125. Further studies on the rôle of the hypophysis in the metabolism of carbohydrates. The autonomic control of the pituitary gland. (With L. H. Weed [1] and C. Jacobson [3]) *Johns Hopk. Hosp. Bull.,* Feb. 1913, 24: 40–52.

⟨Presented at the meeting of the American Physiological Society, Cleveland, December 30, 1912. Abstract: *Amer. J. Physiol.,* 1912–13, 31: xiii–xiv.

126. Robert Fletcher, 1823–1912. *Boston med. surg. J.,* Feb. 27, 1913, 168: 330.

127. Concerning the symptomatic differentiation between disorders of the two lobes of the pituitary body: with notes on a syndrome accredited to hyperplasia of the anterior and secretory stasis or insufficiency of the posterior lobe. *Amer. J. med. Sci.,* March 1913, 145: 313–328.

⟨Read in the Symposium on Internal Secretions at the meeting of the American Medical Association, held at Atlantic City, June 1912.

128. Concerning diabetes insipidus and the polyurias of hypophysial origin. *Boston med. surg. J.,* June 19, 1913, 168: 901–910. Also: *Med. Commun. Mass. med. Soc.,* 1913, 24: 23–49.

⟨The Shattuck Lecture. Delivered at the annual meeting of the Massachusetts Medical Society on June 10, 1913.

129. Hibernation and the pituitary body. (With E. Goetsch) *Proc. Soc. exp. Biol., N.Y.,* 1913, 11: 25–26. See No. 149.

130. The pars anterior and its relation to the reproductive glands. (With E. Goetsch [1]) *Proc. Soc. exp. Biol., N.Y.,* 1913, 11: 26–27.

131. Operative experiences with lesions of the pituitary body. *Trans. Amer. surg. Ass.,* 1913, 31: 467–468.

132. Realignments in greater medicine: their effect upon surgery and the influence of surgery upon them. *Brit. med. J.,*

Aug. 9, 1913, 2: 290–297. Also: *Lancet,* Aug. 9, 1913, 2: 369–375.
¶General address in surgery delivered to the XVIIth International Congress of Medicine, at its meeting in London on August 7, 1913. In No. 15.

133. The correlation of the organs of internal secretion and their disturbances. *Lancet,* Aug. 23, 1913, 2: 546–547.
¶Report of paper given at the joint session of the Section of Medicine and the Section of Physiology at the XVIIth International Congress of Medicine, August 8, 1913.

134. The treatment of tumours of the brain and the indications for operation. *Lancet,* Aug. 23, Sept. 6, 1913, 2: 552, 739.
¶Report of paper given at the joint session of the Section of Surgery with the Section of Neuropathology, XVIIth International Congress of Medicine, August 11, 1913.

135. Affections of the pituitary body. *Lancet,* Aug. 23, 1913, 2: 565.
¶Report of a paper given at the XVIIth International Congress of Medicine on August 9, 1913.

136. Psychic disturbances associated with disorders of the ductless glands. *Amer. J. Insan.,* 1913, 69: 965–990.
¶Address delivered at the opening exercises of the Henry Phipps Psychiatric Clinic, Johns Hopkins Hospital, Baltimore, Md., April 16–18, 1913.

137. Experiences with the meningeal fibro-endothelioma. *J. nerv. ment. Dis.,* 1913, 40: 41–44.
¶Report of meeting of the New York Neurological Society, November 12, 1912.

138. The perimetric deviations accompanying pituitary lesions (preliminary note). *J. nerv. ment. Dis.,* 1913, 40: 793–794.
¶Report at 39th annual meeting of the American Neurological Association, held in Washington, May 5–7, 1913.

1914

139. Studies on the cerebro-spinal fluid and its pathway. I. Introduction. *J. med. Res.,* Sept. 1914, n.s. 26: 1–19.
¶This is the first of a series of nine papers on the physiology of the cerebrospinal fluid. The others are listed below as follows: Nos. 640–645, 143, 153.

140. Surgical experiences with pituitary disorders. *J. Amer. med. Ass.,* Oct. 31, 1914, 63: 1515–1525.

⟨This paper formed the basis of the eighth Weir Mitchell Lecture, before the College of Physicians of Philadelphia, February 25, 1914.

141. The quatercentenary of Andreas Vesalius. 1514– December 31—1914. *Boston med. surg. J.*, Dec. 31, 1914, 171: 995–1002.

142. A centripetal *versus* a centrifugal hospital service. In [pp. 22–31]: *Peter Bent Brigham Hospital, Boston, Founder's Day, November 12, 1914.* Boston: Privately printed [1914], 31 pp.
⟨Address, on behalf of the staff, on Founder's Day.

1915

143. Studies on cerebro-spinal fluid. VIII. The effect of pituitary extract upon its secretion (choroidorrhoea). (With L. H. Weed [1]) *Amer. J. Physiol.*, Jan. 1915, 36: 77–103.

144. Concerning the results of operations for brain tumor. *J. Amer. med. Ass.*, Jan. 16, 1915, 64: 189–195.
⟨An amplification of a discussion of Prof. Küttner's paper, "The results in one hundred operations performed on the diagnosis of brain tumor," read before the Section on Surgery at the 65th annual meeting of the American Medical Association in Atlantic City, June 23, 1914.

145. Portraits of Vesalius. *Med. Rec., N.Y.*, Feb. 6, 1915, 87: 246–247.
⟨Given at annual meeting of the New York Academy of Medicine, January 7, 1915.

146. Distortions of the visual fields in cases of brain tumour. (Fourth paper) Chiasmal lesions, with especial reference to bitemporal hemianopsia. (With C. B. Walker) *Brain*, March 1915, 37: 341–400.

147. From an ambulance surgeon's diary. *Harv. Alumni Bull.*, May 26, 1915, 17: 608–610.

148. The Harvard Unit at the American Ambulance in Neuilly, Paris. *Boston med. surg. J.*, May 27, 1915, 172: 801–803.

149. Hibernation and the pituitary body. (With E. Goetsch) *J. exp. Med.*, July 1, 1915, 22: 25–47.

150. Tumors of the brain and meninges. In: *Osler's Modern medicine.* Philadelphia: Lea & Febiger, 1915, 2nd ed., 5: 308–350. British edition: *A system of medicine* (Osler and McCrae). London: Oxford University Press, 1915, 2nd ed., 5: 308–350.

151. Hydrocephalus. In: *Osler's Modern medicine*. Philadelphia: Lea & Febiger, 1915, 2nd ed., 5: 351–358. British edition: *A system of medicine* (Osler and McCrae). London: Oxford University Press, 1915, 2nd ed., 5: 351–358.

152. The work of the American Ambulance Hospital in Paris. *Privately printed*, 8 pp.

〖Printed and circulated by Robert Bacon as an appeal for further funds [October 1, 1915].

153. Studies on the cerebro-spinal fluid and its pathway. No. IX. Calcareous and osseous deposits in the arachnoidea. (With L. H. Weed) *Johns Hopk. Hosp. Bull.*, Nov. 1915, 26: 367–372.

154. Report of the Surgeon-in-Chief. In: *First annual report of the Peter Bent Brigham Hospital for the years 1913 and 1914*. Cambridge, Mass., 1915, 41–113.

1916

155. Hereditary anchylosis of the proximal phalangeal joints (symphalangism). *Genetics*, Jan. 1916, 1: 90–106.

〖A preliminary note appeared under the same title in: *Proc. nat. Acad. Sci., Wash.*, Dec. 1915, 1: 621–622, after being presented to the Academy, October 30, 1915; see also *J. nerv. ment. Dis.*, 1916, 43: 445–446, for report of presentation before Boston Society of Psychiatry and Neurology, November 18, 1915.

156. Headache. *Boston med. surg. J.*, March 2, 1916, 174: 325–327.

〖Abstract by A. Gregg of a lecture delivered at the Harvard Medical School on January 28, 1916.

157. With the British Medical Corps in France. *Yale Rev.*, April 1916, 5: 523–539.

〖In No. 15; see also Nos. 22, 23.

158. Concerning operations for the cranio-cerebral wounds of modern warfare. *Milit. Surg.*, June 1916, 38: 601–615; July 1916, 39: 22–30.

〖Presented in substance before the American Philosophical Society, Philadelphia, April 14, 1916, and based on experiences in the American Ambulance at Neuilly-sur-Seine.

159. Yale in medicine. In: *The book of the Yale pageant*. New Haven: Yale Univ. Press, 1916, 150–154.

160. Studies of optic-nerve atrophy in association with chiasmal lesions. (With C. B. Walker [1]) *Arch. Ophthal., N.Y.*, Sept. 1916, 45: 407–437.

161. On convulsive spasm of the face produced by cerebello-pontine tumors. *J. nerv. ment. Dis.*, Oct. 1916, 44: 312–321.
⟨Read at the 42nd annual meeting of the American Neurological Association, May 8–10, 1916.

162. Anosmia and sellar distension as misleading signs in the localization of a cerebral tumor. *J. nerv. ment. Dis.*, Nov. 1916, 44: 415–423.
⟨Read at the 42nd annual meeting of the American Neurological Association, May 8–10, 1916.

163. Report of the Surgeon-in-Chief. In: *Second annual report of the Peter Bent Brigham Hospital*. Cambridge, Mass., 1916, 44–108.

1917

164. Experiences with acoustic tumors. *Johns Hopk. Hosp. Bull.*, July 1917, 28: 238–240.
⟨Abstract of paper given before the Johns Hopkins Hospital Medical Society, February 5, 1917.

165. The bombing of the Harvard Base Hospital. *Harv. Alumni Bull.*, Oct. 25, 1917, 20: 80–83.

166. Fractures of the skull. Meninges, ependyma, and brain. Parts 1 and 2 of Chapter I (Surgery of the head) [pp. 7–84] in: *War surgery of the nervous system. A digest of the important medical journals and books published during the European War*. War Department, Office of the Surgeon-General. Washington: Govt. Printing Office, 1917. 8vo, 360 pp.
⟨In the preface to the volume it is stated that "for the brain, we have used the chapters from Keen's *Surgery* written by Dr. Harvey Cushing." See No. 93.

Tumors of the nervus acusticus. See No. 3.

1918

167. Distortions of the visual fields in cases of brain tumor. (Fifth paper) Chiasmal lesions, with especial reference to homonymous hemianopsia with hypophyseal tumor. (With C. B. Walker [1]) *Arch. Ophthal., N.Y.*, March 1918, 47: 119–145.

168. Notes on penetrating wounds of the brain. *Brit. med. J.*, Feb. 23, 1918, 1: 221–226.

169. A study of a series of wounds involving the brain and

its enveloping structures. *Brit. J. Surg.*, April 1918, 5: 558–684.

⟨This is Dr. Cushing's principal paper on the repair of war wounds of the head. It is generally regarded as the most important contribution on neurosurgery of the war period.

1919

170. Considérations sur les plaies pénétrantes du cerveau. *Arch. Méd. Pharm. milit.*, 1919, 71: 665–668.

⟨Report given at the "5ᵉ Conférence chirurgicale interalliée pour l'étude des plaies de guerre, 21 novembre 1918."

171. Concerning "Harvard Units." [Letter to the Editor] *Boston med. surg. J.*, April 3, 1919, 180: 403.

172. Concerning the establishment of a National Institute of Neurology. *Amer. J. Insan.*, Oct. 1919, 76: 113–129. Also: *Trans. Amer. med.-psychol. Ass.*, 1919, 26: 167–183.

⟨Annual address before the 75th annual meeting of the American Medico-Psychological Association, Philadelphia, June 18–20, 1919.

173. Neurological surgery and the war. *Boston med. surg. J.*, Nov. 6, 1919, 181: 549–552.

⟨Read before the annual meeting of the Massachusetts Medical Society, June 4, 1919.

174. Some neurological aspects of reconstruction. *Arch. Neurol. Psychiat., Chicago*, Nov. 1919, 2: 493–504. Also: *Trans. Amer. neurol. Ass.*, 1919, 24–35; *Trans. Congr. Amer. Phys. Surg.*, 1919, 11: 23–41.

⟨Read at the XIth Triennial Session of the Congress of American Physicians and Surgeons, Atlantic City, N.J., June 16, 1919, at a symposium on the subject of Medical and Surgical Reconstruction. For abstract, see *Med. Rec., N.Y.*, July 19, 1919, 96: 125–126.

The Story of U.S. Army Base Hospital No. 5. See No. 5.

175. Abstracts in: *Manual of neuro-surgery*. Washington: Govt. Printing Office, 1919, 492 pp. [pp. 119–149] Fractures of the skull. Part I from Keen's *Surgery* (see No. 93). [pp. 217–229] Steps of suboccipital operation. From *Tumors of the nervus acusticus* (see No. 3).

1920

176. List of publications from the Surgical Department of the Peter Bent Brigham Hospital and the Laboratory of Surgical Research, Harvard Medical School, 1912–1919. [*Boston: Privately printed*, 1920], 12 pp.

177. Introduction to [pp. v-xxii]: *The old humanities and the new science.* By Sir William Osler, Bt., M.D., F.R.S. Boston and New York: Houghton Mifflin Co., 1920. xxii, 64 pp.

178. The purpose and technical steps of a subtemporal decompression. In: *Surgical diagnosis and treatment.* By American Authors. A. J. Ochsner, Ed. Philadelphia: Lea & Febiger, 1920, 1: 407–448.

179. Brain tumor statistics. *Med. Rec., N.Y.,* March 6, 1920, 97: 417–418.

❡A stenographer's note of remarks at the Clinical Congress of the American College of Surgeons held in New York, October 21, 1919. Paper never published.

180. William Osler the man. *Ann. med. Hist.* [Summer No., 1919 (delayed publication)], 1920, 2: 157–167.

❡An amplification of a note on Sir William Osler which appeared anonymously in the *Boston Evening Transcript,* Jan. 3, 1920. In No. 15.

181. Report of the Surgeon-in-Chief. In: *Sixth annual report of the Peter Bent Brigham Hospital for the year 1919.* Cambridge, Mass., 1920, 54–150.

182. Alterations of intracranial tension by salt solutions in the alimentary canal. (With F. E. B. Foley) *Proc. Soc. exp. Biol. N.Y.,* May 22, 1920, 17: 217–218.

183. Remarks on the acoustic neuromas and on ethmoidal operations for choked disc. *Trans. Amer. laryng. rhin. otol. Soc.,* 1920, 129–135.

❡Remarks before the American Laryngological, Rhinological and Otological Society, Harvard Medical School, June 4, 1920.

184. Two cases of splenectomy for splenic anemia. A clinical lecture, Jan. 21, 1920, to third-year students, telling an old story. *And* A report on the pathologic changes in splenic anemia (written in 1900, but not published), by W. G. MacCallum. *Arch. Surg., Chicago,* July 1920, 1: 1–22.

185. Accessory sinus disease and choked disk. *J. Amer. med. Ass.,* July 24, 1920, 75: 236–237.

186. The major trigeminal neuralgias and their surgical treatment based on experiences with 332 Gasserian operations. First paper. The varieties of facial neuralgia. *Amer. J. med. Sci.,* Aug. 1920, 160: 157–184.

❡This paper and one published elsewhere (see No. 187) on the treatment of trigeminal neuralgia formed the basis of the Nathan Lewis

Hatfield Lecture before the College of Physicians of Philadelphia, December 16, 1919.

187. The rôle of deep alcohol injections in the treatment of trigeminal neuralgia. *J. Amer. med. Ass.*, Aug. 14, 1920, 75: 441–443.
⟨This paper formed a section of the Nathan Lewis Hatfield Lecture (see No. 186).

188. Biography of Sir William Osler. [Note.] *Ann. med. Hist.* [Fall No., 1919], 1920, 2: 303.
⟨Appeal for letters or information.

189. Funeral services of General William Crawford Gorgas and Lord Fisher. *Boston med. surg. J.*, Sept. 2, 1920, 183: 315–316.
⟨Reprinted from letter to the Editor, *Boston Evening Transcript* of July 31, 1920.

190. Discussion on perimetric methods. *Brit. J. Ophthal.*, Oct. 1920, 4: 467–470.
⟨Given at the Oxford Ophthalmological Congress, July 15, 1920.

191. The special field of neurological surgery after another interval. *Arch. Neurol. Psychiat., Chicago*, Dec. 1920, 4: 603–637. Also: *Illinois med. J.*, Feb.–March 1921, 39: 133–141, 185–195; *Wis. med. J.*, March 1921, 19: 501–520; *J. Iowa St. med. Soc.*, Sept.–Nov. 1921, 11: 337–342, 385–394, 426–430; *Ohio St. med. J.*, May–June 1921, 17: 293–302, 373–380.
⟨This address was made to do double duty before the Tri-State District Medical Society at Waterloo, Iowa, October 7, 1920, and the Cleveland Academy of Medicine, October 8, 1920.

192. Cerebral surgery. *Trans. Amer. neurol. Ass.*, 1920, p. 141.

1921

193. Report of the Surgeon-in-Chief. In: *Seventh annual report of the Peter Bent Brigham Hospital for the year 1920*. Cambridge, Mass., 1921, 50–113.

194. Further concerning the acoustic neuromas. *Laryngoscope*, April 1921, 31: 209–228.
⟨Remarks before the New England Otological and Laryngological Society meeting at the Peter Bent Brigham Hospital, November 18, 1920.

195. Boston Society of Psychiatry and Neurology. Meeting

at the Peter Bent Brigham Hospital, January 20, 1921. *Arch. Neurol. Psychiat., Chicago,* June 1921, 5: 743–756.

196. Disorders of the pituitary gland. Retrospective and prophetic. *J. Amer. med. Ass.,* June 18, 1921, 76: 1721–1726.

¶Presidential address before the Association for the Study of Internal Secretions, Boston, June 6, 1921. See also: Trastornos de la hipofisis. Ojeada retrospectiva y perspectiva. *J. Amer. med. Ass.* (Edición en Español), July 1, 1921, 6: 1–6.

197. Address at [Yale] Alumni meeting, New Haven, June 21, 1921. *Yale Alumni Weekly,* July 8, 1921, 30: 1103–1104.

198. The personality of a hospital. *Boston med. surg. J.,* Nov. 3, 1921, 185: 529–538.

¶Ether Day Address, Massachusetts General Hospital, October 18, 1921. Exercises in celebration of the centennial of the opening of the Hospital and the seventy-fifth anniversary of Ether Day. Also issued in book form (Boston, 1930, 8vo, 40 pp.), to be "given to all graduating from the Massachusetts General Hospital in memory of Dr. and Mrs. Samuel Parkman by their daughter Mrs. W. W. Vaughan." In No. 15.

199. Remarks at conferring of honorary fellowships in the Royal College of Surgeons in Ireland. *Surg. Gynec. Obstet.,* Dec. 1921, 33: 707–708.

¶Ninth convocation of the American College of Surgeons, held in Philadelphia, October 28, 1921.

200. Prefatory note [pp. 739–742] to: Dedication exercises of the Oscar C. Tugo Circle, Pasteur and Longwood Avenues, Boston, October 18, 1921, in memory of the first enlisted man in the American Expeditionary Force to be killed in the Great War. *Boston med. surg. J.,* Dec. 22, 1921, 185: 739–746.

¶This was issued in book form: *Boston: Privately printed (Merrymount Press)* 1922. 8vo, 34 pp., 3 pl. [Prefatory note, pp. 1–12.] Here the title is slightly different, the end reading: "to be killed by the enemy."

201. Distortions of the visual fields in cases of brain tumor. (Sixth paper) The field defects produced by temporal lobe lesions. *Trans. Amer. neurol. Ass.,* 1921, 374–420. (Discussion, pp. 420–423) Also: *Brain,* Jan. 1922, 44: 341–396.

¶Presented before the American Neurological Association, Atlantic City, June 14, 1921.

1922

202. Report of the Surgeon-in-Chief. In: *Eighth annual report of the Peter Bent Brigham Hospital for the year 1921.* Cambridge, Mass., 1922, 52–105.

203. A large epidermal cholesteatoma of the parieto-temporal region deforming the left hemisphere without cerebral symptoms. *Surg. Gynec. Obstet.,* May 1922, 34: 557–566.

❡Case presented to the Boston Society of Psychiatry and Neurology at a meeting at the Peter Bent Brigham Hospital, January 20, 1921.

204. Les syndromes hypophysaires au point de vue chirurgical. *Rev. neurol.,* June 1922, 38: 779–808.

❡Presented at the IIIe Réunion Neurologique Internationale Annuelle, Paris, June 2–3, 1922. Translated into French by P. Martin.

205. The cranial hyperostoses produced by meningeal endotheliomas. *Arch. Neurol. Psychiat., Chicago,* Aug. 1922, 8: 139–152. Also: *Trans. Amer. neurol. Ass.,* 1922, 53–68.

❡Presented before the American Neurological Association, at the 48th annual meeting, held at Washington, D.C., May 2–4, 1922.

206. William Stewart Halsted, 1852–1922. *Science,* Oct. 27, 1922, 56: 461–464. Also: *Proc. Amer. Acad. Arts Sci.,* Sept. 1923, 58: 599–604. (In No. 24a)

207. The meningiomas (dural endotheliomas): their source, and favoured seats of origin. *Brain,* Oct. 1922, 45: 282–316. Also: *West London med. J.,* 1922, 27: 109–143. Also as originally illustrated and delivered: Boston: Privately printed, 1922, 40 pp.

❡The Cavendish Lecture, delivered before the West London Medico-Chirurgical Society, June 13, 1922. Abstracted in: *Brit. med. J.,* June 24, 1922, 1: 1001–1002. Also: *Med. Pr.,* Sept. 6, 20, 1922, n.s. 114: 199–202; 242–245.

208. The physician and the surgeon. *Boston med. surg. J.,* Nov. 2, 1922, 187: 623–630. Also: *Surg. Gynec. Obstet.,* Dec. 1922, 35: 701–710.

❡Presidential address before the American College of Surgeons, Boston, October 27, 1922. In No. 15.

209. Remarks on the bestowal of the Henry Jacob Bigelow Medal to Dr. W. W. Keen. *Boston med. surg. J.,* Nov. 2, 1922, 187: 650.

210. Laboratories: then and now. In: The opening of the Biological Building of McGill University. [*Montreal: Privately printed*], 1922, 13–25.

❡An address given October 5, 1922, at the dedication of the New Biological Laboratories of McGill University, Montreal. Abstracted in: *Canad. med. Ass., J.,* Jan. 1923, 13: 59–61.

1923

211. Report of the Surgeon-in-Chief. In: *Ninth annual re-*

port of the Peter Bent Brigham Hospital for the year 1922.
Cambridge, Mass., 1923, 50–98.

212. Surgical end-results in general, with a case of cavernous haemangioma of the skull in particular. *Surg. Gynec. Obstet.,* March 1923, 36: 303–308.
¶Presidential address before the Clinical Congress of the American College of Surgeons, Boston, October 23, 1922.

213. Louisa Parsons, first superintendent of nurses in the University of Maryland Hospital. *Univ. Hosp. Nurses' Alumnae Bull.,* April 1923, 3: 3–11.
¶An address given in connection with the presentation of Miss Parsons' medals and decorations to the University Hospital Training School on the dedication of its new Nurses' Home, Baltimore, November 16, 1922. In No. 15.

214. Contributions to the clinical study of intracranial aneurysms. *Guy's Hosp. Rep.,* April 1923, 73: 159–163.

215. Primary gliomas of the chiasm and optic nerves in their intracranial portion. (With P. Martin [1]) *Arch. Ophthal., N.Y.,* May 1923, 52: 209–241.
¶The basis of a clinical demonstration before the New England Ophthalmological Society held at the Peter Bent Brigham Hospital, November 20, 1922.

216. The "Boston Tins." *Boston med. surg. J.,* July 5, 1923, 189: 8–12.
¶An address before the New England Surgical Dressings Committee in connection with the unveiling of a tablet at the Peter Bent Brigham Hospital, on May 25, 1923, in commemoration of the Committee's work. In No. 15.

217. Xanthochromia and increased protein in the spinal fluid above tumors of the cauda equina. (With J. B. Ayer) *Arch. Neurol. Psychiat., Chicago,* Aug. 1923, 10: 167–193.

218. Neurological surgeons: with the report of one case. *Arch. Neurol. Psychiat., Chicago,* Oct. 1923, 10: 381–390. Also: *Trans. Amer. neurol. Ass.,* 1923, 1–10.
¶Presidential address at the 49th annual meeting of the American Neurological Association, Boston, May 31, 1923.

219. Notes on a series of intracranial tumors and conditions simulating them. Tumor suspects; tumors unverified; tumors verified. *Arch. Neurol. Psychiat., Chicago,* Dec. 1923, 10: 605–668.
¶The basis of a clinic before the American Neurological Association at the Peter Bent Brigham Hospital, Boston, May 31, 1923.

1924

220. List of publications from the Surgical Department of the Peter Bent Brigham Hospital and the Laboratory of Surgical Research, Harvard Medical School, 1912–1923. *Cambridge, Mass.: Univ. Press* [1924], 23 pp.

221. The clinical teacher and the medical curriculum. *J. Amer. med. Ass.*, March 15, 1924, 82 : 841–844.

⟨Read before the Annual Congress on Medical Education, Medical Licensure, Public Health and Hospitals, Chicago, March 3, 1924. See also: O professor de clinica e o curriculum medico. *Sao Paulo Med.*, Aug. 1934, 7 : 67–80. Reprinted in part: *School Life* (Washington, D.C.), April 1924, 9 : 169–170; 187–188. In No. 15.

222. George H. Simmons: editor, publisher and writer. In [pp. 7–16]: *George H. Simmons. A testimonial.* Chicago: American Medical Association, 1924, 41 pp.

⟨Testimonial banquet with presentation of portrait to Dr. George Henry Simmons on the twenty-fifth anniversary as editor of the *Journal of the American Medical Association*, Monday, the ninth of June, 1924. (H.C. was Toastmaster on this occasion.)

Les tumeurs du nerf auditif. See No. 4.

223. Report of the Surgeon-in-Chief. In: *Tenth annual report of the Peter Bent Brigham Hospital for the year 1923.* Cambridge, Mass., 1924, 62–109.

224. The Western Reserve and its medical traditions. *Cleveland: Privately printed* [1924], 33 pp.

⟨An address at the dedication of the New Medical Building of Western Reserve University, October 9, 1924. In No. 15.

225. Medulloblastoma cerebelli: a common type of mid-cerebellar glioma of childhood. (With P. Bailey [1]) *Trans. Amer. neurol. Ass.*, 1924, 89–121. Also: *Arch. Neurol. Psychiat., Chicago.* Aug. 1925, 14, 192–223.

⟨Presented at the fiftieth annual meeting of the American Neurological Association, Philadelphia, June 5, 1924.

226. Papillomas of the choroid plexus, with the report of six cases. (With L. E. Davis [1]) *Trans. Amer. neurol. Ass.*, 1924, 365–394. Also: *Arch. Neurol. Psychiat., Chicago,* June 1925, 13 : 681–710.

⟨Presented before the American Neurological Association, Philadelphia, June 7, 1924.

1925

227. Microchemical color reactions as an aid to the identifi-

cation and classification of brain tumors. (With P. Bailey [1]) *Proc. nat. Acad. Sci.*, Jan. 1925, 11: 82–84.
⟨Read before the Academy, November 12, 1924.

228. Discussion of [pp. 10–11]: Roentgenological aspects of brain tumors—meningiomas. By M. C. Sosman and T. J. Putnam. *Amer. J. Roentgenol.*, Jan. 1925, 13: 1–12.
⟨Read at the 25th annual meeting, American Roentgen Ray Society, Swampscott, Mass., Sept. 3–6, 1924.

229. John Irvine Hunter, 1897–1924. *Boston Med. Surg. J.*, Jan. 29, 1925, 192: 214–215.

230. Should Boston have a community chest? [Editorial.] *Boston Traveler,* Jan. 31, 1925, p. 16.

231. Robert Williamson Lovett, 1859–1924. *Boston med. surg. J.*, Feb. 19, 1925, 192: 374–375.
⟨Transcript of a minute adopted by the Boston Surgical Society, July 2, 1924.

232. Experiences with blood replacement during or after major intracranial operations. (With L. E. Davis [1]) *Surg. Gynec. Obstet.*, March 1925, 40: 310–322.
⟨Presented before the Clinical Congress of the American College of Surgeons, New York, October 21, 1924.

233. An eclipse observed over two centuries ago. *Harv. Alumni Bull.*, March 5, 1925, 27: 669–671.

The life of Sir William Osler. See Nos. 6, 7.

234. Experimentum periculosum: judicium difficile. *Yale Alumni Weekly,* March 27, April 3, 1925, 34: 801–803; 835–836. Also: *Science,* April 10, 1925, 61: 373–379.
⟨An address at the dedication of the Sterling Hall of Medicine, Yale University, February 23, 1925. In No. 15.

235. Report of the Surgeon-in-Chief. In: *Eleventh annual report of the Peter Bent Brigham Hospital for the year 1924.* Boston, 1925, 69–117.

236. Prefatory note [pp. 329–333] to: Chronic subdural hematoma. Its pathology, its relation to pachymeningitis hemorrhagica and its surgical treatment. By T. J. Putnam. With cases contributed by members of the Society of Neurological Surgeons. *Arch. Surg., Chicago,* Sept. 1925, 2: 329–393.

237. Prefatory note [pp. 314–316] to: A consideration of the

hypophysial adenomata. By N. M. Dott and P. Bailey. *Brit. J. Surg.,* Oct. 1925, 13: 314–366.

238. The third circulation and its channels. (Cameron Lecture, abridged) *Lancet,* Oct. 24, 1925, 209: 851–857.

239. The pituitary gland as now known. (Cameron Lecture, abridged) *Lancet,* Oct. 31, 1925, 209: 899–906.

240. Intracranial tumours and the surgeon. (Cameron Lecture, abridged) *Lancet,* Nov. 7, 1925, 209: 956–962.
¶For this and two preceding items see No. 10.

241. Ductless glands (discussion). *Trans. Congr. Amer. Phys. Surg.,* 1925, 13: 61–64.
¶Read at the XIIIth Triennial Session of the Congress of American Physicians and Surgeons, Washington, D.C., May 5 and 6, 1925.

242. Foreword [pp. x–xi] to: M. H. Spielmann's *Iconography of Andreas Vesalius.* London: John Bale, Sons & Danielsson, Ltd., 1925. 8vo, xxxvii, 243 pp.

243. Introduction [pp. 7–12] to: Facsimile edition of Canano's *Musculorum humani corporis picturata dissectio.* (Ferrara 1541?) Annotated by H. C. and E. C. Streeter. Florence: R. Lier & Co., 1925. 8vo, 47 pp.+facsimile.

1926

A classification of the tumors of the glioma group, etc. (With P. Bailey [1]) See No. 8.

Studies in intracranial physiology and surgery. See No. 10.

244. Report of the Surgeon-in-Chief. In: *Twelfth annual report of the Peter Bent Brigham Hospital for the year 1925.* Boston, 1926, 68–117.

245. Consecratio medici. *J. Amer. med. Ass.,* Aug. 21, 1926, 87: 539–542.
¶Commencement address at the Jefferson Medical College, Philadelphia, June 5, 1926. In No. 15.

246. The value of books to the medical profession. *Med. J. Rec.,* Dec. 1, 1926, 124: 712–713.
¶Address delivered at the dinner (November 17, 1926) in honor of the newly elected honorary fellows preceding the formal opening exercises (November 18) in dedication of the New York Academy of Medicine. Also [under title of *Books and the doctor*]: *Bull. N.Y. Acad. Med.,* Feb. 1927, 2nd ser. 3: 69–72.

1927

247. The doctor and his books. *Cleveland, Ohio: Privately printed* [1927], 26 pp. Also: *Amer. J. Surg.,* Jan. 1928, 4: 100–110.

⟪An address at the opening of the Allen Memorial Medical Library of the Cleveland Medical Library Association, November 13, 1926. In No. 15. Based in part on No. 246.

248. Care of head injuries and injuries to the spine and peripheral nerves in the forward hospitals. In: *Medical Department of the U.S. Army in the World War,* Vol. XI (Surgery), 755–758. Washington: Govt. Printing Office, 1927.

⟪Report of the Senior Consultant in Neurological Surgery, A.E.F., to the Surgeon-General. Submitted December 1918.

249. Diffuse tumors of the leptomeninges: two cases in which the process was revealed only by the microscope. (With C. L. Connor [1]) *Arch. Path. Lab. Med.,* March 1927, 3: 374–392.

250. The intracranial tumors of preadolescence. *Amer. J. Dis. Child.,* April, 1927, 33: 551–584.

⟪Report of a clinic for the combined meeting of the Pediatric Section of the New York Academy of Medicine, the Philadelphia Pediatric Society and the New England Pediatric Society, held at the Peter Bent Brigham Hospital, Boston, October 16, 1926. Also (in part): *Tsinan med. Rev.,* Jan. 1929, 9: 17–24. [Translated into Chinese by T. C. Greene.]

The pathological findings in four autopsied cases of acromegaly, etc. (With L. M. Davidoff) See No. 12.

251. Report of the Surgeon-in-Chief. In: *Thirteenth annual report of the Peter Bent Brigham Hospital for the year 1926.* Cambridge, Mass., 1927, 65–113.

252. The transformation of a malignant paravertebral sympathicoblastoma into a benign ganglioneuroma. (With S. B. Wolbach) *Amer. J. Path.,* May 1927, 3: 203–216.

253. James Ford Rhodes, 1848–1927. In: *Later Years of the Saturday Club, 1870–1920.* M. A. DeWolfe Howe, Ed. Boston: Houghton Mifflin Co., 1927, pp. 346–355. (In No. 24a)

254. Studies in acromegaly. IV. The basal metabolism. (With L. M. Davidoff) *Arch. intern. Med.,* May 1927, 39: 673–697.

255. Letter to *Time. Time,* May 23, 1927, 9: 2.

⟪In answer to paragraph under the caption "Uglies" in issue of May 2, 1927, p. 17.

256. Studies in acromegaly. VI. The disturbances of car-

bohydrate metabolism. (With L. M. Davidoff [1]) *Arch. intern. Med.*, June 1927, 39: 751–779.

257. Experiences with orbito-ethmoidal osteomata having intracranial complications. With the report of four cases. *Surg. Gynec. Obstet.*, June 1927, 44: 721–742.

¶Presidential address before the American Surgical Association, Richmond, Virginia, May 12, 1927. See also: *Trans. Amer. surg. Ass.*, 1927, 45: 1–38.

258. The meningiomas arising from the olfactory groove and their removal by the aid of electro-surgery. *Glasgow: Jackson, Wylie & Co., Publishers to the University*, 1927, 53 pp. Also (in part): *Lancet*, June 25, 1927, 1: 1329–1339.

¶Macewen Memorial Lecture delivered at the University of Glasgow, June 22, 1927.

259. Acromegaly from a surgical standpoint. *Brit. med. J.*, July 2, 9, 1927, 2: 1–9; 48–55. Also: *Trans. med. Soc. Lond.*, 1927, 50: 248–302. Also (in part): *Lancet*, June 18, 1927, 1: 1291–1293.

¶Annual Oration, Medical Society of London, June 13, 1927.

260. Emancipators. *Lancet*, July 23, 1927, 2: 185–186. Also: *Brit. med. J.*, July 30, 1927, 2: 185–186; *Boston med. surg. J.*, Oct. 20, 1927, 197: 651–652; *Health, Mountain View, Calif.*, Feb. 1937, 4: 14–15.

¶An address delivered at the Lister centenary celebration at Edinburgh on July 20, 1927. In No. 15.

261. Presentation of the Henry Jacob Bigelow Medal [to Dr. Rudolph Matas], November 1, 1926. *Boston med. surg. J.*, Oct. 27, 1927, 197: 701.

1928

262. Intracranial tumors. In: *Osler's Modern medicine.* Philadelphia: Lea & Febiger, 1928, 3rd ed., 6: 222–254. British edition: *Modern medicine* (Osler and McCrae). London: Henry Kimpton, 1928, 3rd ed., 6: 222–254.

263. Hydrocephalus. In: *Osler's Modern medicine.* Philadelphia: Lea & Febiger, 1928, 3rd ed., 6: 255–266. British edition: *Modern medicine* (Osler and McCrae). London: Henry Kimpton, 1928, 3rd ed., 6: 255–266.

Tumors arising from the blood-vessels of the brain. (With P. Bailey) See No. 13.

264. Hemangiomas of cerebellum and retina (Lindau's disease). With the report of a case. (With P. Bailey) *Arch. Ophthal., N.Y.*, Sept. 1928, 57: 447–463. Also: *Trans. Amer. ophthal. Soc.*, 1928, 26: 182–202.

❨Presented at the 64th annual meeting of the American Ophthalmological Society, Washington, D.C., June 1928.

265. Report of the Surgeon-in-Chief. In: *Fourteenth annual
report of the Peter Bent Brigham Hospital for the year 1927.*
Boston, 1928, 70–118.

266. The presentation of the Henry Jacob Bigelow Medal,
October 10, 1928 [to Dr. Chevalier Jackson]. *New Engl.
J. Med.,* Oct. 18, 1928, 199: 763.

267. Studies in acromegaly. VII. The microscopical structure
of the adenomas in acromegalic dyspituitarism (fugitive
acromegaly). (With P. Bailey [1]) *Amer. J. Path.,* Nov. 1928,
4: 545–564.

Consecratio medici and other papers. See No. 15.

268. An account of the dedicatory ceremonies in connection
with the Base Hospital No. 5 memorial, October 11, 1928.
Boston: Privately printed [Merrymount Press], 1928, 20 pp.
Also: *Milit. Surg.,* Dec. 1928, 63: 899–901.

269. Electro-surgery as an aid to the removal of intracranial
tumors. With a preliminary note on a new surgical-current
generator by W. T. Bovie, Ph.D., Chicago. *Surg. Gynec.
Obstet.,* Dec. 1928, 47: 751–784.

❨This report marks the introduction of electrosurgical methods in the
removal of intracranial tumors. See also: La electro-cirugía como ele-
mento auxiliar en la extirpación de los tumores intra-craneanos. *Rev.
oto-neuro-oftal.,* Jan. 1929, 4: 1–12.

270. Angioblastic meningiomas. (With P. Bailey [1] and
L. Eisenhardt [3]) *Arch. Path. Lab. Med.,* Dec. 1928, 6:
953–990.

271. Meningiomas arising from the tuberculum sellae: with
the syndrome of primary optic atrophy and bitemporal field
defects combined with a normal sella turcica in a middle-
aged person. (With L. Eisenhardt) *Trans. Sect. Ophthal.
Amer. med. Ass.,* 1928, 322–408. Also: *Arch. Ophthal., Chicago,* Jan., Feb. 1929, 1: 1–41; 168–205.

❨Presented before the Ophthalmological Section of the American
Medical Association, Minneapolis, June 14, 1928.

1929

272. Chronological list of publications from the Surgical De-

partment of the Peter Bent Brigham Hospital and the Laboratory of Surgical Research, Harvard Medical School, 1912–1928. [*Boston: Privately printed*, 1929], 46 pp.

273. Report of the Surgeon-in-Chief. In: *Fifteenth annual report of the Peter Bent Brigham Hospital for the year 1928.* Boston, 1929, 81–129.

274. The medical career. An address on "The ideals, opportunities and difficulties of the medical profession" containing a tribute to Dr. Nathan Smith, founder of the Dartmouth Medical School. *Hanover, N.H.: Dartmouth College,* 1929. 8vo, 53 pp.

⟨Delivered at Dartmouth College, November 20, 1928. Second edition of 500 copies, 1930. In No. 24a.

275. Remarks at the Children's Hospital campaign dinner, March 11, 1929. *C. H. News,* March 15, 1929, 1: 4.

276. Billroth letter. *Orvosképzes* (special Billroth centennial number), April 6, 1929, 19: 1–2.

⟨Letter to Professor Emile de Grósz in connection with the centennial celebration of the birth of Theodor Billroth. Translated into Hungarian by Dr. de Grósz, *ibid.,* 487.

277. Exercises in celebration of the bicentenary of the birth of John Hunter. *New Engl. J. Med.,* April 18, 1929, 200: 810–823.

⟨A brief account of the exercises before the Harvard Medical Society, held at the Peter Bent Brigham Hospital, December 11, 1928, when the principal speakers were Dr. Leroy M. S. Miner, Dr. William Pearce Coues, Dr. Arlie V. Bock, Dr. Frederic T. Lewis, and Professor William M. Wheeler, with H.C. presiding. A display of Hunter's editions, English and American, with portraits and Hunteriana of various kinds was arranged by Dr. Henry Viets.

278. The chiasmal syndrome of primary optic atrophy and bitemporal field defects in adult patients with a normal sella turcica. *Trans. XIIIth Int. ophthal. Congr.,* Amsterdam, 1929, 97–184.

⟨Read at the Congress, September 12, 1929.

279. The binding influence of a library on a subdividing profession. *Science,* Nov. 22, 1929, 70: 485–491. Also: *Johns Hopk. Hosp. Bull.,* Jan. 1930, 46: 29–42; *Johns Hopk. Nurses Alum. Mag.,* Feb., 1930, 29: 6–19.

⟨Address at the dedication of the William H. Welch Medical Library, Johns Hopkins University, Baltimore, October 17, 1929. In No. 24a.

1930

280. Experiences with the cerebellar medulloblastomas. A critical review. *Acta path. microbiol. scand.*, 1930, 7: 1–86.
❡Read before the Medical Society of Lund, Sept. 4, 1929.

281. William Henry Welch. An anonymous contribution [page 9] to: *The eightieth birthday of William Henry Welch.* New York: Privately printed, Milbank Memorial Fund, 1930, 39 pp. (In No. 24a)

282. Report of the Surgeon-in-Chief. In: *Sixteenth annual report of the Peter Bent Brigham Hospital for the year 1929.* Boston, 1930, 77–132.

283. The separate growth-promoting and gonad-stimulating hormones of the anterior hypophysis: an historical review. (With H. M. Teel [1]) *Endokrinologie,* 1930, 6: 401–420.

284. The chiasmal syndrome. (No. 278 revised and with an additional case.) *Arch. Ophthal., Chicago,* May, June 1930, 3: 505–551; 704–735.

285. Studies in the physiological properties of the growth-promoting extracts of the anterior hypophysis. (With H. M. Teel, [1]) *Endocrinology,* May–June 1930, 14: 157–163.
❡Read before the International Physiological Congress, Boston, August 1929. Abstract in: *Amer. J. Physiol.,* Oct. 1929, 90: 323–324, under title, Concerning the hypophyseal (pars distalis) hormones for growth and for reproductive processes.

286. An American tribute to Sir Anthony Bowlby. *St. Bart's Hosp. J.,* Aug. 1930, 37: 199.
❡Remarks on the occasion of the presentation of a memorial tablet to the Royal College of Surgeons, July 9, 1930.

287. Neurohypophysial mechanisms from a clinical standpoint. *Lancet,* July 19, 26, 1930, 2: 119–127; 175–184.
❡The Lister Memorial Lecture delivered at the Royal College of Surgeons of England, July 9, 1930. Abstract in: *Brit. med. J.,* July 19, 1930, 2: 114–115. In No. 20.

288. Diagnosis of intracranial tumors by supravital technique. (With L. Eisenhardt [1]) *Amer. J. Path.,* Sept. 1930, 6: 541–552. Also: *Trans. Amer. neurol. Ass.,* 1930, 73–88.

Die Gewebs-Verschiedenheit der Hirngliome. See No. 9.

1931

289. Experiences with the cerebellar astrocytomas. A critical review of seventy-six cases. *Surg. Gynec. Obstet.*, Feb. 1931, 52: 129–204.

⟪Basis of second Arthur Dean Bevan Lecture of the Chicago Surgical Society on October 3, 1930, before the joint meeting of the Chicago Surgical Society, the Institute of Medicine of Chicago, the Chicago Neurological Society, the Society of Internal Medicine, the Chicago Pediatric Society, and the Chicago Society of Medical History.

290. Report of the Surgeon-in-Chief. In: *Seventeenth annual report of the Peter Bent Brigham Hospital for the year 1930*. Boston, 1931, 69–106.

291. Eulogy of Major-General Clarence R. Edwards. *Boston Herald*, Feb. 16, 1931, p. 3.

292. A review of Homans' *Textbook of surgery. New Engl. J. Med.*, Feb. 26, 1931, 204: 472–473.

293. Acknowledging reprints. A letter to the Editor. *J. Amer. med. Ass.*, April 4, 1931, 96: 1168.

294. I. The reaction to posterior pituitary extract (pituitrin) when introduced into the cerebral ventricles. II. The similarity in the responses to posterior lobe extract (pituitrin) and to pilocarpine when injected into the cerebral ventricles. III. The action of atropine in counteracting the effects of pituitrin and of pilocarpine injected into the cerebral ventricles. IV. The method of action of pituitrin introduced into the ventricle. V. The counteractive effect of tribromethanol (avertin) on the stimulatory response to pituitrin injected in the ventricle. VI. Concerning a possible "parasympathetic center" in the diencephalon. *Proc. nat. Acad. Sci.*, April, May 1931, 17: 163–180; 239–264.

⟪These six papers provided the basis of the William Henry Welch Lecture, *The posterior pituitary hormone and the parasympathetic nervous system*, delivered at the Mount Sinai Hospital, New York, April 30, 1931. In No. 20.

295. One hundred and fifty years. From tallow-dip to television. *New Engl. J. Med.*, June 11, 1931, 204: 1235–1244.

⟪The Annual Discourse before the Massachusetts Medical Society at the 150th reunion held in Boston, June 8–10, 1931. Translated into Rumanian: O suta cincizeci de ani. Dela lumînarea de său la televiziune. *Insemnari iesene, Iaşi* 1938, 7: 82–104. In No. 24a.

296. George Strong Derby, 1875–1931. *New Engl. J. Med.*, Dec. 24, 1931, 205: 1262–1264. (In No. 24a)

297. The surgical mortality percentages pertaining to a series of two thousand verified intracranial tumors. Standards of computation. *Trans. Amer. neurol. Ass.*, 1931, 456–463. Also: *Arch. Neurol. Psychiat.*, *Chicago*, June 1932, 27: 1273–1280. ⟨Read at the fifty-seventh annual meeting of the American Neurological Association at Boston, May 1931. This paper represents the last portion of a communication made at the International Neurological Congress in Bern, September 1931. The mortality statistics for tumors of different kinds and situations, separately considered, which form the basis of these tables, were published elsewhere in monograph form (see No. 16).

1932

298. The basophil adenomas of the pituitary body and their clinical manifestations (pituitary basophilism). *Johns Hopk. Hosp. Bull.*, March 1932, 50: 137–195.
The subject matter of this paper was presented at the New York Academy of Medicine, January 5, 1932; at the Yale Medical School, February 24, 1932, and before the Johns Hopkins Hospital Medical Society, February 29, 1932. Abstracted in: *J. nerv. ment. Dis.*, July, 1932, 76: 50–56. In No. 20.

299. Remarks at the presentation of the Henry Barton Jacobs Collection to the Welch Medical Library, January 14, 1932. *Johns Hopk. Hosp. Bull.*, May 1932, 50: 307–309.

Intracranial tumours. See No. 16.

300. Bemerkungen über eine Serie von 2000 verifizierten Gehirntumoren mit der dazugehörigen chirurgischen Mortalitätsstatistik. *Chirurg*, 1932, 4: 254–265.
⟨Presented at the International Neurological Congress in Bern, 1931. Translated, with alterations, from No. 297, by C. F. List.

301. Peptic ulcers and the interbrain. *Surg. Gynec. Obstet.*, July 1932, 55: 1–34.
⟨The basis of the fourth Balfour Lecture given at the University of Toronto, April 8, 1931. A letter from Dr. Cushing concerning the work of Schiassi on the subject of neurogenic ulceration of the gastrointestinal tract was published (Italian translation) in: *Policlinico* (sez. prat.) 1933, 40: 1977. In No. 20.

302. Further concerning a parasympathetic center in the interbrain. VII. The effect of intraventricularly injected histamine. VIII. The comparative effects on gastric motility of intramuscular and intraventricular pituitrin, pilocarpine and histamine. *Proc. nat. Acad. Sci.*, July 1932, 18: 500–510. In No. 20.

303. Further notes on pituitary basophilism. *J. Amer. med. Ass.*, July 23, 1932, 99: 281–284. In No. 20.

304. Report of the Surgeon-in-Chief. In: *Eighteenth annual report of the Peter Bent Brigham Hospital for the year 1931.* Boston, 1932, 74–111.

305. The specific dynamic action of protein in patients with pituitary disease. (With M. N. Fulton [1]) *Arch. intern. Med.,* Nov. 1932, 50: 649–667.

Papers relating to the pituitary body, hypothalamus, and parasympathetic nervous system. See No. 20.

1933

306. Concerning a hypothalamic center for parasympathetic impulses. *Arch. Sci. biol., Napoli,* Jan. 1933, 18: 107–109.

⟨Report at the XIVth International Physiological Congress, Rome, September 1932.

307. "Dyspituitarism": twenty years later. With special consideration of the pituitary adenomas. *Arch. intern. Med.,* April 1933, 51: 487–557.

⟨The Harvey Society Lecture, as given in part, January 19, 1933, at the New York Academy of Medicine. Also: *Harvey Lect.,* 1932–1933, 90–158.

308. Homo chirurgicus. *New Engl. J. Med.,* May 4, 1933, 208: 922–929.

⟨Given before the Boston Surgical Society, May 3, 1933, on the occasion of the bestowal of the Henry Jacob Bigelow Medal.

309. Medicine at the crossroads. *J. Amer. med. Ass.,* May 20, 1933, 100: 1567–1575. Also: *Trans. Cong. Amer. Phys. Surg.,* 1933, 15: 1–24.

⟨Presidential address, read before the XVth Congress of Physicians and Surgeons at Washington, D.C., May 9, 1933. In No. 24a.

310. William Thomas Councilman, January 1, 1854–May 26, 1933. *Science,* June 30, 1933, 77: 613–618. Also (with bibliography): *Biogr. Mem. nat. Acad. Sci.,* 1937, 18: 157–174. (In No. 24a)

311. In honor of Professor Elihu Thomson. *Science,* July 14, 1933, 78: 24–26. Also [pp. 59–63]: *Elihu Thomson eightieth birthday celebration.* [Cambridge, Mass.:] Technology Press, 1933, 80 pp.

⟨Address "on behalf of scientific professions other than engineering" at the dinner celebrating Dr. Thomson's eightieth birthday, at the Massachusetts Institute of Technology, May 1, 1933.

312. Posterior pituitary activity from an anatomical standpoint. *Amer. J. Path.*, Sept. 1933, 9: 539–547.

1934

313. Hyperactivation of the neurohypophysis as the pathological basis of eclampsia and other hypertensive states. *Amer. J. Path.*, March 1934, 10: 145–175.
¶These studies, made in the Surgical Laboratory of the Peter Bent Brigham Hospital with the assistance of Dr. Louise Eisenhardt, were the basis of the first lecture before the Medical Research Society delivered at University College, London, November 2, 1933. Abstract of report before the National Academy of Sciences, April 25, 1933: *Proc. Soc. exp. Biol.*, N.Y., June 1933, 30: 1424–1425.

314. Experimental pituitary basophilism. (With K. W. Thompson [1]) *Proc. roy. Soc.*, May 1934, 115 B: 88–100.

315. The Doctors Welch of Norfolk. *New Engl. J. Med.*, May 24, 1934, 210: 1132–1134. (In No. 24a)

316. The pioneer medical schools of Central New York. [*Syracuse, N.Y.: Privately printed*], 1934, 36 pp.
¶An address at the centenary celebration of the College of Medicine of Syracuse University, June 4, 1934. In No. 24a.

317. From a surgeon's journal. I. The Harvard Unit and the Ambulance Américaine. II. The battle of Boston Common. III. With the B.E.F. in France. IV. With the A.E.F. *Atlantic Monthly*, Oct.–Dec. 1934, 154: 385–399; 590–601; 696–707; Jan. 1935, 155: 102–116.
¶See also Nos. 22, 23.

1935

318. Psychiatrists, neurologists and the neurosurgeon. *Yale J. Biol. Med.*, Jan. 1935, 7: 191–207. Also [pp. 17–36]: *Neurological biographies and addresses*. London: Oxford University Press, 1936, 178 pp.
¶An address at the opening ceremonies of the Montreal Neurological Institute at McGill University, September 27, 1934. In No. 24a.

319. The humanizing of science. *Science*, Feb. 8, 1935, 81: 137–143. Also: *Diplomate*, April 1935, 7: 115–124.
¶Presidential address before the History of Science Society, Washington, December 28, 1934. Under the caption, "Science, the Runaway Horse," reprinted in part in *Boston Globe*, March 11, 1935. In No. 24a.

320. William Beaumont's rendezvous with fame. *Yale J. Biol. Med.*, Dec. 1935, 8: 113–126.

¶An address given in Lebanon, Connecticut, June 1, 1935, at the dedication of the Beaumont Memorial Highway in connection with the tercentennial celebration of the first settlement in Connecticut. In No. 24a.

Intrakranielle Tumoren. See No. 18.

1936

321. Ivan Pavlov. *Soviet Russia Today,* April 1936, p. 9.

322. Prefatory note [p. 421] to: The ultimate results of operations for intracranial tumours. A study of a series of cases after a nine-year interval. By H. Cairns. *Yale J. Biol. Med.,* May 1936, 8: 421–492. Also in part: *Lancet,* May 30, June 6, 1936, 1: 1223–1228; 1291–1294; translated by F. K. Kessel: *Nervenarzt,* 1936, 9: 401–410. See also No. 19.

323. A bibliographical study of the Galvani and the Aldini writings on animal electricity. (With J. F. Fulton [1]) *Ann. Sci.,* July 1936, 1: 239–268.

From a surgeon's journal. See Nos. 22, 23.

324. Corrigenda and addenda to "The life of Sir William Osler." *Oxford: University Press,* 1936, 8 pp. See No. 6.

1937

325. Ercole Lelli and his écorché. *Yale J. Biol. Med.,* Jan. 1937, 9: 199–213. Also: *Proc. Charaka Cl.,* 1938, 9: 3–20.
¶First read at the meeting of the American Association for the Advancement of Science, Atlantic City, December 28, 1932. Read before the Charaka Club, February 20, 1935. Also given on October 9, 1936 before the Beaumont Medical Club.

326. Perry Williams Harvey, 1869–1932. Books and the man. *Yale Univ. Libr. Gaz.,* Jan. 1937, 11: 43–52.
¶An address at the Sterling Memorial Library on December 5, 1936, at the opening of an exhibition of the Baskervilles collected by Mr. Harvey and given to Yale by the members of his family. In No. 24a.

327. Inhibition of action of pituitary hormones by animal sera. (With K. W. Thompson [1]) *Proc. roy. Soc.,* Jan. 1937, 121 B: 501–517.

328. Remarks at Alumni luncheon, Yale University, 23 June 1937. In part: *Yale Alumni Weekly,* July 9, 1937, 46: 23.

Tumeurs intracraniennes. See No. 19.

329. Toast given at luncheon, Association for Research in Nervous and Mental Disease, New York, December 27, 1937. Reported in part: *New York Times,* December 28, 1937.

1938

330. Notes on the first reasonably successful removal of an intracranial tumor. (With L. Eisenhardt) *Bull. Los Angeles neurol. Soc.,* Sept. 1938, 3: 95–98.

Meningiomas. (With L. Eisenhardt) See No. 24.

1939

330a. The Mayo brothers and their clinic. *Science,* Sept. 8, 1939, 90: 225–226. (In No. 24a)

330b. Response at seventieth birthday dinner. In: *Harvey Cushing's seventieth birthday party, April 8, 1939. Speeches, letters and tributes.* Springfield, Ill.: Charles C Thomas, 1939, xii, 148 pp.

330c. The Society of Clinical Surgery in retrospect. (In press)

❡Read for Dr. Cushing at the 68th meeting of the Society of Clinical Surgery, Nashville, Tenn., April 14 and 15, 1939.

1940

The medical career and other papers. See No. 24a.

IV. PAPERS FROM DR. CUSHING'S CLINICS AND LABORATORIES

331. ALPERS, B. J.   A study of one hundred and two ventricular fluids in cases of brain tumor. *Amer. J. Psychiat.*, Jan. 1925, 4: 509–519.

332. ARMITAGE, G.   Osteoma of the frontal sinus: with particular reference to its intracranial complications, and with the report of a case. *Brit. J. Surg.*, April 1931, 18: 565–580.

333. ARMITAGE, G., and MEAGHER, R.   Gliomas of the corpus callosum. *Z. ges. Neurol. Psychiat.*, 1933, 146: 454–488.

AYER, J. B.   See No. 217.

334. BAGDASAR, D.   Le traitement chirurgical des gommes cérébrales. *Rev. neurol.*, July 1929, 2: 1–30.

BAGDASAR, D.   See also No. 360.

335. BAILEY, P.   Contribution to the histopathology of "pseudotumor cerebri." *Arch. Neurol. Psychiat.*, *Chicago*, Oct. 1920, 4: 401–416.

336. BAILEY, P.   Cruveilhier's "tumeurs perlées." *Surg. Gynec. Obstet.*, Oct. 1920, 31: 390–401.

337. BAILEY, P.   Concerning the clinical classification of intracranial tumors. *Arch. Neurol. Psychiat.*, *Chicago*, April 1921, 5: 418–437.

338. BAILEY, P.   Cytological observations on the pars buccalis of the hypophysis cerebri of man, normal and pathological. *J. med. Res.*, June–Sept. 1921, 42: 349–381.

339. BAILEY, P.   Note concerning keratin and keratohyalin in tumors of the hypophysial duct. *Ann. Surg.*, Oct. 1921, 74: 501–505.

340. BAILEY, P.   Die Funktion der Hypophysis cerebri. *Ergebn. Physiol.*, 1922, 20: 162–206.

341. BAILEY, P.   Recent developments in electrodiagnosis. *Arch. Neurol. Psychiat.*, *Chicago*, April 1923, 9: 436–449.

342. BAILEY, P.   A new principle applied to the staining of the fibrillary neuroglia. *J. med. Res.*, Sept. 1923, 44: 73–77.

343. BAILEY, P.   A study of tumors arising from ependymal cells. *Arch. Neurol. Psychiat.*, *Chicago*, Jan. 1924, 11: 1–27.

344. BAILEY, P.   Concerning the cerebellar symptoms pro-

duced by suprasellar tumors. *Arch. Neurol. Psychiat., Chicago,* Feb. 1924, 11: 137–150.

345. BAILEY, P. Further observations on pearly tumors. *Arch. Surg., Chicago,* March 1924, 8: 524–534.

346. BAILEY, P. A contribution to the study of aphasia and apraxia. *Arch. Neurol. Psychiat., Chicago,* May 1924, 11: 501–529.

347. BAILEY, P. The results of Roentgen therapy on brain tumors. *Amer. J. Roentgenol.,* Jan. 1925, 13: 48–53.

348. BAILEY, P. Sur un cas de myokymie. *Rev. neurol.,* Jan. 1925, 32: 41–44.

349. BAILEY, P. Quelques nouvelles observations de tumeurs épendymaires. *Ann. Anat. path. méd.-chir.,* Nov. 1925, 10: 481–512.

350. BAILEY, P. Some remarks concerning the platinum chloride method of W. Ford Robertson for the "mesoglia." *Arch. Neurol. Psychiat., Chicago,* March 1927, 17: 420–422.

351. BAILEY, P. Further remarks concerning tumors of the glioma group. *Johns Hopk. Hosp. Bull.,* June 1927, 40: 354–389.

352. BAILEY, P. Sobre el diagnostico de los tumores intracraneales. *Rev. méd. Barcelona,* Nov. 1927, 8: 506–521.

353. BAILEY, P. Histologic atlas of gliomas. *Arch. Path. Lab. Med.,* Dec. 1927, 4: 871–921. Also: *Trans. Amer. neurol. Ass.,* 1927, 107–162.

354. BAILEY, P. The structure of the hypophysis cerebri of man and of the common laboratory mammals. In: *Special Cytology.* E. V. Cowdry, Ed. New York: Paul B. Hoeber, March 1928, 1: 485–499.

355. BAILEY, P. Metastatic tumor in the foot of the left third frontal convolution, with aphasia. *Arch. Neurol. Psychiat., Chicago,* Dec. 1928, 20: 1359–1361.

356. BAILEY, P. Some unusual tumors of the third ventricle. *Bull. N.Y. Acad. Med.,* 2nd series, 1928, 4: 646–655.

357. BAILEY, P. Intracranial sarcomatous tumors of leptomeningeal origin. *Arch. Surg., Chicago,* April 1929, 18: 1359–1402.

358. BAILEY, P. A propos d'une forme spéciale de ménin-

giome angioblastique. *J. Neurol. Psychiat.*, Nov. 1929, 29: 577–581.

359. BAILEY, P.   Further notes on the cerebellar medulloblastomas. The effect of Roentgen radiation. *Amer. J. Path.*, March 1930, 6: 125–136.

360. BAILEY, P., and BAGDASAR, D.   Intracranial chordoblastoma. *Amer. J. Path.*, Sept. 1929, 5: 439–449.

361. BAILEY, P., and BREMER, F.   Experimental diabetes insipidus. *Arch. intern. Med.*, Dec. 1921, 28: 773–803.

362. BAILEY, P., and BUCY, P. C.   Oligodendrogliomas of the brain. *J. Path. Bact.*, Oct. 1929, 32: 735–751.

363. BAILEY, P., and BUCY, P. C.   Astroblastomas of the brain. *Acta psychiat., Kbh.*, 1930, 5: 439–461.

364. BAILEY, P., and DAVIDOFF, L. M.   Concerning the microscopic structure of the hypophysis cerebri in acromegaly. *Amer. J. Path.*, March 1925, 1: 185–207.

365. BAILEY, P., and DAVIS, L. E.   A progressive staining method for mitochondria. *J. med. Res.*, Sept. 1924, 44: 535–538.

366. BAILEY, P., and EISENHARDT, L.   Spongioblastomas of the brain. *J. comp. Neurol.*, Dec. 1932, 56: 391–430.

367. BAILEY, P., and HILLER, G.   The interstitial tissues of the central nervous system: A review. *J. nerv. ment. Dis.*, April 1924, 59: 337–361.

368. BAILEY, P., and MURRAY, H. A.   A case of pinealoma with symptoms suggestive of compulsion neurosis. Clinical report: Dr. Bailey. Psychologic report: Dr. Murray. *Arch. Neurol. Psychiat., Chicago*, May 1928, 19: 932–945.

369. BAILEY, P., and SCHALTENBRAND, G.   Die muköse Degeneration der Oligodendroglia. *Dtsch. Z. Nervenheilk.*, 1927, 97: 231–237.

370. BAILEY, P., SOSMAN, M. C., and VAN DESSEL, A.   Roentgen therapy of gliomas of the brain. *Amer. J. Roentgenol.*, March 1928, 19: 203–264.

371. BAILEY, P., and WOLBACH, S. B.   The histology of tumors of the cerebrum and cerebellum. *J. med. Res.*, Sept. 1923, 44: 104–106.

BAILEY, P.   See also Nos. 8, 9, 13, 225, 227, 237, 264, 267, 270, 448, 449, 450, 510, 511, 579, 580.

372. BANCROFT, F. W., and CROSS, E. S.   Note on the finding of coccidium bigeminum. *Johns Hopk. Hosp. Bull.*, Dec. 1906, 17: 370–372.

BAUER, W.   See No. 380.

373. BEALL, F. C.   Cases of hernia in dogs. *Johns Hopk. Hosp. Bull.*, May 1905, 16: 196–199.

374. BECK, C. S.   A study of lymph pressure. *Johns Hopk. Hosp. Bull.*, July 1924, 35: 206–214.

375. BECK, C. S., and CUTLER, E. C.   A cardiovalvulotome. *J. exp. Med.*, Sept. 1924, 40: 375–379.

376. BECK, C. S., and MOORE, R. L.   The significance of the pericardium in relation to surgery of the heart. *Arch. Surg., Chicago*, Oct. 1925, 11: 550–577.

377. BELT, A. E., and JOELSON, J. J.   The effect of ligation of branches of the renal artery. *Arch. Surg., Chicago*, Jan. 1925, 10: 117–149.

378. BENEDICT, E. B., PUTNAM, T. J., and TEEL, H. M.   Early changes produced in dogs by the injections of a sterile active extract from the anterior lobe of the hypophysis. *Amer. J. med. Sci.*, April 1930, 179: 489–498.

BENEDICT, E.B.   See also Nos. 568, 570.

379. BENEDICT, F. G., and HOMANS, J.   The metabolism of the hypophysectomized dog. *J. med. Res.*, Feb. 1912, 25: 409–502.

380. BENNETT, G. A., BAUER, W., and MADDOCK, S. J.   A study of the repair of articular cartilage and the reaction of normal joints of adult dogs to surgically created defects of articular cartilage, "joint mice," and patellar displacement. *Amer. J. Path.*, Sept. 1932, 8: 499–524.

381. BERNHEIM, B. M.   Experimental surgery of the mitral valve. *Johns Hopk. Hosp. Bull.*, April 1909, 20: 107–110.

382. BERNHEIM, B. M.   A note on some methods of anastomosing blood-vessels. *Johns Hopk. Hosp. Bull.*, April 1909, 20: 116–117.

BERRY, F. B.   See Nos. 388, 389.

383. BIRD, C. E.   Sarcoma complicating Paget's disease of the bone. Report of nine cases, five with pathologic verification. *Arch. Surg., Chicago*, June 1927, 14: 1187–1208.

BISHOP, C. C.   See Nos. 526, 527.

BLACKFAN, K. D. See No. 416.

384. BOOTHBY, W. M. Ether percentages. *J. Amer. med. Ass.*, Sept. 13, 1913, 61: 830–834.

385. BOOTHBY, W. M. The determination of the anaesthetic tension of ether vapor in man, with some theoretical deductions therefrom, as to the mode of action of the common volatile anaesthetics. *J. Pharmacol.*, March 1914, 5: 379–392.

386. BOOTHBY, W. M. A determination of the circulation rate in man at rest and at work. *Amer. J. Physiol.*, May 1915, 37: 383–417.

387. BOOTHBY, W. M. The clinical value of metabolic studies of thyroid cases. *Boston med. surg. J.*, Oct. 19, 1916, 175: 564–566.

388. BOOTHBY, W. M., and BERRY, F. B. The effect of work on the percentage of haemoglobin and number of red corpuscles in the blood. *Amer. J. Physiol.*, May 1915, 37: 378–382.

389. BOOTHBY, W. M., and BERRY, F. B. Distension of the lungs: Its effect on the respiration in man and in normal and vagotomized dogs. *Amer. J. Physiol.*, May 1915, 37: 433–451.

390. BOOTHBY, W. M., and PEABODY, F. W. A comparison of methods of obtaining alveolar air. *Arch. intern. Med.*, March 1914, 13: 497–506.

391. BOOTHBY, W. M., and SANDIFORD, I. The calibration of the Waller gas balance and the Connell anaesthetometer. *J. Pharmacol.*, March 1914, 5: 369–378.

392. BOOTHBY, W. M., and SANDIFORD, I. The analysis of nitrous oxide for physiological work. *Amer. J. Physiol.*, May 1915, 37: 371–377.

393. BOOTHBY, W. M., and SANDIFORD, I. The tension of carbon dioxide and oxygen in the venous blood at rest and at work. *Amer. J. Physiol.*, March 1916, 40: 1–2.

394. BOOTHBY, W. M., and SHAMOFF, V. N. A study of the late effect of division of the pulmonary branches of the vagus nerve on the gaseous metabolism, gas exchange and respiratory mechanism in dogs. *Amer. J. Physiol.*, May 1915, 37: 418–432.

BORDLEY, J., JR. See Nos. 92, 96, 97, 106.

BOVIE, W. T. See No. 269.

BOWIE, M. A. See Nos. 564, 565.

BRANCH, J. R. B. See No. 86.

395. BREMER, F. Global aphasia and bilateral apraxia due to an endothelioma compressing the gyrus supramarginalis. *Arch. Neurol. Psychiat., Chicago,* June 1921, 5: 663–669.

396. BREMER, F. Contribution à l'étude de la physiologie du cervelet. La fonction inhibitrice du paléo-cérébellum. *Arch. int. Physiol.,* July 15, 1922, 19: 189–226.

BREMER, F. See also No. 361.

BRENIZER, A. G. See No. 432.

397. BRIGGS, J. B. The results of some observations on blood-pressure in morbid conditions in adults. *Johns Hopk. Hosp. Bull.,* Feb. 1903, 14: 35–37.

398. BRIGGS, J. B., and COOK, H. W. The value of an accurate knowledge of arterial blood pressure to the clinician. *Maryland med. J.,* 1903, 46: 1–13.

399. BRYAN, A. H., and GAISER, D. W. The influence of diet and the anterior pituitary growth hormone on the growth rate of adolescent rats. *Amer. J. Physiol.,* Jan. 1932, 99: 379–390.

400. BRYANT, C. H. Primary sarcoma of the heart in a dog. *Johns Hopk. Hosp. Bull.,* Dec. 1907, 18: 474–476.

401. BUCKLEY, R. C. Tissue culture studies of the glioblastoma multiforme. *Amer. J. Path.,* Sept. 1929, 5: 467–472.

402. BUCKLEY, R. C. Pontile gliomas. A pathologic study and classification of twenty-five cases. *Arch. Path. Lab. Med.,* April 1930, 9: 779–819.

403. BUCKLEY, R. C. Intracerebral calculi. Report of a case. *Arch. Neurol. Psychiat., Chicago,* June 1930, 23: 1203–1211.

404. BUCKLEY, R. C., and DEERY, E. M. Abnormality of the cerebrum and leptomeninges simulating an intracranial tumor. *Amer. J. Path.,* Sept. 1929, 5: 459–465.

405. BUCKLEY, R. C., and EISENHARDT, L. Study of a meningioma in supravital preparations, tissue culture and paraffin sections. *Amer. J. Path.,* Nov. 1929, 5: 659–664.

BUCKLEY, R. C. See also Nos. 442, 512.

BUCY, P. C. See Nos. 362, 363.

BYSSHE, S. M. See No. 528.

406. CAIRNS, H. Observations on the localisation of intra-

cranial tumours: The disclosure of localising signs following decompression or ventriculography. *Lancet,* March 23, 1929, 1: 600–603. Also: *Arch. Surg., Chicago,* April 1929, 18: 1936–1944.

407. CAIRNS, H. A study of intracranial surgery. *Spec. Rep. Ser. med. Res. Coun.,* Lond., No. 125, 1929, 83 pp.

CAIRNS, H. See also No. 322.

CAMMANN, A. See No. 9.

CARR, G. L. See No. 474.

408. CHURCHMAN, J. W. Prostatic hypertrophy and prostatic atrophy in the dog. *Johns Hopk. Hosp. Bull.,* Dec. 1907, 18: 463–464.

409. COBB, S. Haemangioma of the spinal cord, associated with skin naevi of the same metamere. *Ann. Surg.,* Dec. 1915, 62: 641–649.

COHEN, S. S. See No. 49.

CONNOR, C. L. See No. 249.

410. COOK, H. W. The clinical value of blood-pressure determinations as a guide to stimulation in sick children. *Johns Hopk. Hosp. Bull.,* Feb. 1903, 14: 37–38.

COOK, H. W. See also No. 398.

COOMBS, H. I. See No. 617.

CROSS, E. S. See No. 372.

411. CROWE, S. J. The parasites of Baltimore dogs. *Johns Hopk. Hosp. Bull.,* Dec. 1907, 18: 464–467.

412. CROWE, S. J. On the excretion of hexamethylenamin (urotropin) in the bile and pancreatic juice. *Johns Hopk. Hosp. Bull.,* April 1908, 19: 109–113. Also: *Arch. int. Pharmacodyn.,* 1908, 18: 315–325.

413. CROWE, S. J. On the excretion of hexamethylenamin (urotropin) in the cerebrospinal fluid and its therapeutic value in meningitis. *Johns Hopk. Hosp. Bull.,* April 1909, 20: 102–105. Also: *Therapist,* 1909, 19: 77.

414. CROWE, S. J. Hexamethylenamin in the treatment of systemic infections with a special emphasis upon its use as a prophylactic. *Johns Hopk. Hosp. Bull.,* Sept. 1912, 23: 255–263.

CROWE, S. J. See also Nos. 100, 107, 111.

CUTLER, E. C.   See Nos. 375, 600.

415. DANDY, W. E.   The nerve supply to the pituitary body. *Amer. J. Anat.*, Nov. 1913, 15: 333–343.

416. DANDY, W. E., and BLACKFAN, K. D.   An experimental and clinical study of internal hydrocephalus. *J. Amer. med. Ass.*, Dec. 1913, 61: 2216–2217. Also: *Beitr. klin. Chir.*, 1914, 93: 392–486.

417. DANDY, W. E., and GOETSCH, E.   The blood supply of the pituitary body. *Amer. J. Anat.*, Jan. 1911, 11: 137–150.

418. DAVIDOFF, L. M.   Studies in acromegaly. II. Historical note. *Endocrinology*, Sept.–Oct. 1926, 10: 453–460.

419. DAVIDOFF, L. M.   Studies in acromegaly. III. The anamnesis and symptomatology in one hundred cases. *Endocrinology*, Sept.–Oct. 1926, 10: 461–483.

DAVIDOFF, L. M.   See also Nos. 12, 254, 256, 364, 460, 461, 462, 463.

420. DAVIS, L. E.   A physio-pathologic study of the choroid plexus with the report of a case of villous hypertrophy. *J. med. Res.*, Sept. 1924, 44: 521–534.

421. DAVIS, L. E.   Decerebrate rigidity in man. *Arch. Neurol. Psychiat., Chicago*, May 1925, 13: 569–579.

DAVIS, L. E.   See also Nos. 226, 232, 365.

422. DAVIS, S. G.   On the effect of narcosis upon the body temperature. *Johns Hopk. Hosp. Bull.*, April 1909, 20: 118–125.

423. DEERY, E. M.   Note on calcification in pituitary adenomas. *Endocrinology*, Sept.–Oct., 1929, 13: 455–458.

424. DEERY, E. M.   Syndromes of tumors in the chiasmal region. A review of one hundred and seventy cases receiving a transfrontal operation. *J. nerv. ment. Dis.*, April 1930, 71: 383–396.

DEERY, E. M.   See also No. 404.

DENIKER, M.   See No. 4.

DERGE, H. F.   See No. 536.

DIAL, D. E.   See No. 523.

DIONNE, M. J.   See No. 594.

425. DOCHEZ, A. R.   A further report on hernia in dogs. *Johns Hopk. Hosp. Bull.*, Dec. 1906, 17: 380–383.

DOCK, W. See No. 478.

DOTT, N. M. See No. 237.

426. DRINKER, C. K., and HURWITZ, S. H. The factors of coagulation in primary pernicious anaemia. *Arch. intern. Med.*, May 1915, 15: 733–745.

DRINKER, C. K. See also No. 515.

427. DRURY, D. W. Aural acuity and brain lesions. I. Audiometric studies. *Ann. Otol. etc., St. Louis,* Sept. 1931, 40: 682–709.

DUNPHY, J. E. See No. 618.

EDSON, P. J. See No. 595.

428. EISENHARDT, L. The operative mortality in a series of intracranial tumors. *Arch. Surg., Chicago,* April 1929, 18: 1927–1935.

429. EISENHARDT, L. Diagnosis of intracranial tumors by supravital technique. Further studies. *Arch. Neurol. Psychiat., Chicago,* Aug. 1932, 28: 299–319.

430. EISENHARDT, L. Long postoperative survivals in cases of intracranial tumor. *Res. Publ. Ass. nerv. ment. Dis.,* Dec. 1935, 16: 390–416.

EISENHARDT, L. See also Nos. 24, 270, 271, 288, 313, 330, 366, 405, 549, 556.

431. ELKIN, D. C. Cirsoid aneurism of the scalp, with the report of an advanced case. *Ann. Surg.,* Sept. 1924, 80: 332–340.

EMERSON, L. E. See No. 475.

432. EVANS, H. M., and BRENIZER, A. G. Notes on the resection of large portions of the small intestine. *Johns Hopk. Hosp. Bull.,* Dec. 1907, 18: 477–480.

433. FARIS, C. M. Two cases of haemorrhagic cyst of the thyroid gland. *Johns Hopk. Hosp. Bull.,* May 1905, 16: 180–184.

FINNEY, J. M. T. See No. 30.

434. FLEMING, L. N., and MARVIN, F. W. Familial fibromyxomata of the peripheral nerves; a report of three cases. *Surg. Gynec. Obstet.,* March 1917, 24: 287–295.

435. FOLEY, F. E. B. Clinical uses of salt solution in condi-

tions of increased intracranial tension. *Surg. Gynec. Obstet.,* Aug. 1921, 33: 126–136.

436. FOLEY, F. E. B. Alterations in the currents and absorption of cerebrospinal fluid following salt administration. *Arch. Surg., Chicago,* March 1923, 6: 587–604.

437. FOLEY, F. E. B. An instrument and method for aseptic anastomosis of the intestine. *Surg. Gynec. Obstet.,* June 1923, 36: 836–839.

438. FOLEY, F. E. B., and PUTNAM, T. J. The effect of salt ingestion on cerebro-spinal fluid pressure and brain volume *Amer. J. Physiol.,* Oct. 1920, 53: 464–476.

FOLEY, F. E. B. See also No. 182.

439. FRIED, B. M. Sarcomatosis of the brain. *Arch. Neurol. Psychiat., Chicago,* Oct. 1925, 14: 563–564. Also: *Ibid.,* Feb. 1926, 15: 205–217.

440. FRIED, B. M. The origin of histiocytes (macrophages) in the lungs. An experimental study by the use of intratracheal injections of vital stain. *Arch. Path. Lab. Med.,* May 1927, 3: 751–767.

441. FRIED, B. M. Metastatic inoculation of a meningioma by cancer cells from a bronchiogenic carcinoma. *Amer. J. Path.,* Jan. 1930, 6: 47–52.

442. FRIED, B. M., and BUCKLEY, R. C. Primary carcinoma of the lungs. IV. Intracranial metastases. *Arch. Path. Lab. Med.,* Feb., 1930, 9: 483–527.

443. FRIED, B. M., and WHITAKER, L. R. The effect of liver damage on cholecystography in dogs by the use of sodium tetraiodophenolphthalein. *Arch. intern. Med.,* March 1926, 37: 388–397.

444. FRIED, B. M., and WHITAKER, L. R. Intratracheal injection of iodized oil. Experimental studies. *Arch. intern. Med.,* Nov. 1927, 40: 726–739.

445. FULTON, J. F. El reflejo rotuliano. *Rev. med. Barcelona,* Dec. 1927, 8: 582–590.

446. FULTON, J. F. Observations upon the vascularity of the human occipital lobe during visual activity. *Brain,* Sept. 1928, 51: 310–320.

447. FULTON, J. F. Vasomotor and reflex sequelae of unilateral cervical and lumbar ramisectomy in a case of Raynaud's

disease, with observations on tonus. *Ann. Surg.*, Nov. 1928, 88: 827–841.

448. FULTON, J. F., and BAILEY, P. Some clinical observations upon the physiology of the hypothalamus. *Amer. J. Physiol.*, June 1928, 85: 372.

449. FULTON, J. F., and BAILEY, P. Contribution to the study of tumors in the region of the third ventricle: their diagnosis and relation to pathological sleep. *J. nerv. ment. Dis.*, Jan., Feb. and March 1929, 69: 1–25; 145–164; 261–277.

450. FULTON, J. F., and BAILEY, P. Nueva contribución sobre los tumores del tercer ventrículo. Su asociación con el sindrome de Recklinghausen y con el edema de Quincke. *Arch. argent. Neurol.*, Aug. 1929–Jan. 1930, 5: 1–27.

FULTON, J. F. See also Nos. 323, 522.

FULTON, M. N. See No. 305.

GAGNON, J. See No. 607.

GAISER, D. W. See Nos. 399, 619.

451. GATCH, W. D. The radical cure of prolapsus vaginae. *Johns Hopk. Hosp. Bull.*, Dec. 1906, 17: 374–377.

452. GERAGHTY, J. T. Balano-posthitis in dogs. *Johns Hopk. Hosp. Bull.*, Dec. 1907, 18: 462–463.

453. GIBBS, F. A. Intracranial tumor with unequal choked disk. Relationship between the side of greater choking and the position of the tumor. *Arch. Neurol. Psychiat.*, *Chicago*, April 1932, 27: 828–835.

454. GIBBS, F. A. Frequency with which tumors in various parts of the brain produce certain symptoms. *Arch. Neurol. Psychiat.*, *Chicago*, Nov. 1932, 28: 969–989.

GILMAN, P. K. See No. 79.

455. GOETSCH, E. The influence of pituitary feeding upon growth and sexual development. An experimental study. *Johns Hopk. Hosp. Bull.*, Feb. 1916, 27: 29–50.

456. GOETSCH, E. Functional significance of mitochondria in toxic thyroid adenomata. *Johns Hopk. Hosp. Bull.*, May 1916, 27: 129–133.

457. GOETSCH, E. The occurrence of gastric mucosa in a case of Meckel's diverticulum producing intestinal obstruction. *Johns Hopk. Hosp. Bull.*, June 1919, 30: 143–161.

GOETSCH, E.   See also Nos. 113, 119, 129, 130, 149, 417.

458. GRANT, F. C.   Concerning intracranial malignant metastases: their frequency and the value of surgery in their treatment. *Ann. Surg.*, Nov. 1926, 84: 635–646.

459. GRANT, F. C.   Cerebellar symptoms produced by supratentorial tumors. A further report. *Arch. Neurol. Psychiat., Chicago,* Aug. 1928, 20: 292–308.

460. GRAVES, R. C., and DAVIDOFF, L. M.   The choice of pyelographic mediums. *J. Amer. med. Ass.*, Jan. 20, 1923, 80: 168–171.

461. GRAVES, R. C., and DAVIDOFF, L. M.   Studies on the ureter and bladder with especial reference to regurgitation of the vesical contents. *J. Urol.*, Sept. 1923, 10: 185–231.

462. GRAVES, R. C., and DAVIDOFF, L. M.   II. Studies on the ureter and bladder with especial reference to regurgitation of the vesical contents. *J. Urol.*, Aug. 1924, 12: 93–103.

463. GRAVES, R. C., and DAVIDOFF, L. M.   III. Studies on the bladder and ureters with especial reference to regurgitation of the vesical contents. Regurgitation as observed in cats and dogs. *J. Urol.*, July 1925, 14: 1–17.

464. GREENE, T. C.   The ability to localize sound. A study of binaural hearing in patients with tumor of the brain. *Arch. Surg., Chicago,* April 1929, 18: 1825–1841.

GREENE, T. C.   See also No. 250.

GREGG, A.   See No. 156.

465. GREY, E.   Observations on the protective enzymes of the body (Abderhalden). *Johns Hopk. Hosp. Bull.*, April 1914, 25: 117–122.

466. GREY, E.   Studies on the localization of cerebellar tumors. I. Significance of staggering gait, limb ataxia, the Romberg test, and adiadochokinesis. *J. nerv. ment. Dis.*, Oct. 1915, 42: 670–679.

467. GREY, E.   Studies on the localization of cerebellar tumors. III. Posterior new growths without nystagmus. *J. Amer. med. Ass.*, Oct. 16, 1915, 65: 1341–1345.

468. GREY, E.   Fibrin as a haemostatic in cerebral surgery. *Surg. Gynec. Obstet.*, Oct. 1915, 21: 452–454.

469. GREY, E.   Experimental study of the effect of cholecystgastrostomy on gastric acidity. *J. exp. Med.*, Jan. 1, 1916, 23: 15–24.

470. GREY, E. Studies on localization of cerebellar tumors. II. The position of the head and suboccipital discomforts. *Ann. Surg.*, Feb. 1916, 63: 129–139.

471. GREY, E. On localization of function in the canine cerebellum. *J. nerv. ment. Dis.*, Feb. 1916, 43: 105–120.

472. GREY, E. Studies on the localization of cerebellar tumors. IV. Pointing reaction and caloric test. *Amer. J. med. Sci.*, May 1916, 151: 693–705.

473. GREY, E. Studies on the localization of cerebellar tumors. V. The cranial nerves. *Johns Hopk. Hosp. Bull.*, Sept. 1916, 27: 251–262.

474. GREY, E., and CARR, G. L. An experimental study of the factors responsible for non-infectious bone atrophy. *Johns Hopk. Hosp. Bull.*, Nov. 1915, 26: 381–385.

475. GREY, E., and EMERSON, L. E. A striking acquirement of visualizing power and the development of dreams following a cerebral tumor extirpation. *J. Amer. med. Ass.*, Dec. 13, 1913, 61: 2141–2145.

GRÓSZ, E. See No. 276.

476. GUNDRUM, F. F. Osteo-sarcoma of the radius in a dog. *Johns Hopk. Hosp. Bull.*, Dec. 1907, 18: 467–469.

HAGGART, W. W. See No. 537.

HAIGHT, C. See No. 513.

477. HARRISON, P. W. An effort to determine the sensory path from the ocular muscles. *Johns Hopk. Hosp. Bull.*, April 1909, 20: 113–116.

478. HARRISON, T. R., DOCK, W., and HOLMAN, E. Experimental studies in arteriovenous fistulae: cardiac output. *Heart*, Dec. 1924, 11: 337–341.

479. HARVEY, S. C. Congenital variations in the peritoneal relations of the ascending colon, caecum, appendix and terminal ileum. *Ann. Surg.*, June 1918, 67: 641–686.

480. HARVEY, S. C. Fibrin paper as an haemostatic agent. *Ann. Surg.*, July 1918, 67: 67–71.

HARVEY, S. C. See also No. 591.

HELMHOLZ, H. F. See Nos. 73, 77.

481. HENDERSON, W. R. Sexual dysfunction in adenomas of the pituitary body. *Endocrinology*, March–April 1931, 15: 111–127.

482. HENRY, G. R. Chronic endocarditis with bloody ascites. *Johns Hopk. Hosp. Bull.*, Dec. 1906, 17: 372–374.

483. HEUER, G. J. Observations on distemper. *Johns Hopk. Hosp. Bull.*, Dec. 1906, 17: 385–393.

HEUER, G. J. See also Nos. 120, 122.

HILLER, G. See No. 367.

484. HOEN, T. I. The choroid plexus as a dialyzing membrane. I. Observations in experimental hydrocephalus. *Arch. Neurol. Psychiat.*, Chicago, Sept. 1931, 26: 496–500.

485. HOLMAN, E. Experimental studies in arteriovenous fistulas. I. Blood volume variations. *Arch. Surg.*, Chicago, Nov. 1924, 9: 822–836.

486. HOLMAN, E. Experimental studies in arteriovenous fistulas. III. Cardiac dilatation and blood vessel changes. *Arch. Surg.*, Chicago, Nov. 1924, 9: 856–879.

487. HOLMAN, E., and KOLLS, A. C. Experimental studies in arteriovenous fistulas. II. Pulse and blood pressure variations. *Arch. Surg.*, Chicago, Nov. 1924, 9: 837–855.

HOLMAN, E. See also No. 478.

488. HOMANS, J. Degeneration of the islands of Langerhans associated with experimental diabetes in the cat. *J. med. Res.*, March 1914, 30: 49–68.

HOMANS, J. See also Nos. 107, 111, 379.

489. HOPKINS, J. G. Six cases of infection with filaria immitis. *Johns Hopk. Hosp. Bull.*, Dec. 1906, 17: 377–379.

490. HORRAX, G. Studies on the pineal gland. I. Experimental observations. *Arch. intern. Med.*, May 1916, 17: 607–626.

491. HORRAX, G. Studies on the pineal gland. II. Clinical observations. *Arch. intern. Med.*, May 1916, 17: 627–645.

492. HORRAX, G. Intracranial aërocele following fractured skull. *Ann. Surg.*, Jan. 1921, 73: 19–23.

493. HORRAX, G. Contributions of the war to the physiology of the nervous system. *Physiol. Rev.*, April 1921, 1: 269–294.

494. HORRAX, G. The surgery of gunshot wounds of the skull and brain. In: *Oxford Surgery*. New York: Oxford University Press, 1921, V: 581–614.

495. HORRAX, G. Diseases of the pituitary gland. In: *Oxford Medicine*. New York: Oxford University Press, 1921, III: 805–828.

496. HORRAX, G.   Xanthochromia due to acute, purulent spinal meningitis. *Arch. Neurol. Psychiat., Chicago*, July 1922, 8: 24–26.

497. HORRAX, G.   A consideration of the dermal versus the epidermal cholesteatomas having their attachment in the cerebral envelopes. *Arch. Neurol. Psychiat., Chicago*, Sept. 1922, 8: 265–285.

498. HORRAX, G.   Clinical syndromes involving the pineal gland. In: *Endocrinology and metabolism*. L. F. Barker, Ed. New York: D. Appleton and Co., 1922, II: 49–56.

499. HORRAX, G.   Visual hallucinations as a cerebral localizing phenomenon, with especial reference to their occurrence in tumors of the temporal lobes. *Arch. Neurol. Psychiat., Chicago*, Nov. 1923, 10: 532–545.

500. HORRAX, G.   Generalized cisternal arachnoiditis simulating cerebellar tumor. *Trans. Amer. med. Ass.*, 1923, 210–231.

501. HORRAX, G.   Generalized cisternal arachnoiditis simulating cerebellar tumor: its surgical treatment and end-results. *Arch. Surg., Chicago*, July 1924, 9: 95–112.

502. HORRAX, G.   The significance of papilledema to the neurological surgeon. *Arch. Ophthal., N.Y.*, March 1925, 54: 130–141.

503. HORRAX, G.   Present day considerations of brain tumors. *N. Y. St. Med. J.*, March 1, 1926, 26: 186–189.

504. HORRAX, G.   Differential diagnosis of tumors primarily pineal and primarily pontile. *Arch. Neurol. Psychiat., Chicago*, Feb. 1927, 17: 179–190.

505. HORRAX, G.   Surgery of the brain. In: *Nelson Loose-Leaf Surgery*. New York: Thomas Nelson & Sons, 1927, II: 349–418.

506. HORRAX, G.   Experiences with cordotomy. *Arch. Surg., Chicago*, April 1929, 18: 1140–1164.

507. HORRAX, G.   The pineal body. In: *Oxford Medicine*. New York: Oxford University Press, 1930, III: 1017–1026.

508. HORRAX, G.   Brain surgery. In: *Nelson Loose-Leaf Surgery*. New York: Thomas Nelson & Sons, Oct. 1931, 435–438.

509. HORRAX, G.   Head injuries and some of their complications. *Amer. J. Surg.*, Oct. 1932, 18: 1–15; 18.

510. HORRAX, G., and BAILEY, P. Tumors of the pineal body. *Arch. Neurol. Psychiat., Chicago,* April 1925, 13 : 423–467.

511. HORRAX, G., and BAILEY, P. Pineal pathology. Further studies. *Arch. Neurol. Psychiat., Chicago,* March 1928, 19 : 394–413.

512. HORRAX, G., and BUCKLEY, R. C. A clinical study of the differentiation of certain pontile tumors from acoustic tumors. *Arch. Neurol. Psychiat., Chicago,* Dec. 1930, 24 : 1217–1230.

513. HORRAX, G., and HAIGHT, C. A study of the recession of choked disks following operations for brain tumor. *Arch. Ophthal., N.Y.,* Sept. 1928, 57 : 467–473.

514. HORRAX, G., and PUTNAM, T. J. Distortions of the visual fields in cases of brain tumor. (Seventh paper) The field defects and hallucinations produced by tumors of the occipital lobe. *Brain,* 1932, 55 : 499–523.

HOWARD, I. M. See No. 564.

HOWE, M. A. D. See No. 253.

HUNNER, G. L. See No. 33.

515. HURWITZ, S. H., and DRINKER, C. K. The factors of coagulation in the experimental aplastic anemia of benzol poisoning with special reference to the origin of prothrombin. *J. exp. Med.,* May 1, 1915, 21 : 401–424.

HURWITZ, S. H. See also No. 426.

516. JACOBSON, C. A study of the haemodynamic reactions of the cerebrospinal fluid and hypophysial extracts. *Johns Hopk. Hosp. Bull.,* June 1920, 31 : 185–197.

517. JACOBSON, C. A study of the carbohydrate tolerance in Eck fistula and hypophysectomized animals (posterior lobe removal). *Amer. J. Physiol.,* June 1920, 52 : 233–247.

JACOBSON, C. See also Nos. 119, 125.

JOELSON, J. J. See No. 377.

518. JONES, C. Salivary calculus in an acromegalic. *Ann. Surg.,* May 1921, 73 : 527–530.

KEEN, W. W. See No. 93.

KENDALL, L. G. See Nos. 526, 527.

KESSEL, F. K. See Nos. 18, 322.

KEY, J. A.   See No. 654.

KOLLS, A. C.   See No. 487.

519. KRAUSE, W. F., and WHITAKER, L. R.   Effects of different food substances upon emptying of the gall bladder. *Amer. J. Physiol.*, Nov. 1928, 87: 172-179.

520. KREDEL, F. E.   Tissue culture of intracranial tumors: with a note on the meningiomas. *Amer. J. Path.*, July 1928, 4: 337-340.

521. KREDEL, F. E.   Intracranial tumors in tissue culture. *Arch. Surg.*, *Chicago*, April 1929, 18: 2008-2018.

522. KUBIE, L. S., and FULTON, J. F.   A clinical and pathological study of two teratomatous cysts of the spinal cord, containing mucus and ciliated cells. *Surg. Gynec. Obstet.*, Sept. 1928, 47: 297-311.

LANGNECKER, H. L.   See No. 73.

523. LAWRENCE, J. H., and DIAL, D. E.   Effects of intraventricular injection of pituitrin and pilocarpine in dogs. *Proc. Soc. exp. Biol.*, *N.Y.*, Oct. 1932, 30: 49-54.

LAWRENCE, J. S.   See Nos. 544, 596.

LECENE, P.   See No. 43.

524. LEE, F.C.   Some observations on lymph-pressure. *Amer. J. Physiol.*, Feb. 1924, 67: 498-513.

LEE, M. O.   See No. 607.

525. LEHMANN, W.   Zur Frage der Operationsmortalität bei subtentorialen Tumoren. *Arch. klin. Chir.*, 1926, 143: 552-573.

526. LIGHT, R. U., BISHOP, C. C., and KENDALL, L. G.   The production of gastric lesions in rabbits by injection of small amounts of pilocarpine into the cerebrospinal fluid. *J. Pharmacol.*, June 1932, 45: 227-251.

527. LIGHT, R. U., BISHOP, C. C., and KENDALL, L. G.   The response of the rabbit to pilocarpine administered into the cerebrospinal fluid. *J. Pharmacol.*, Jan. 1933, 47: 37-45.

528. LIGHT, R. U., and BYSSHE, S. M.   The administration of drugs into the cerebral ventricles of monkeys: pituitrin, certain pituitary fractions, pitressin, pitocin, histamine, acetyl choline, and pilocarpine. *J. Pharmacol.*, Jan. 1933, 47: 17-36.

529. LIST, C. F.   Die operative Behandlung der Acusticus-

neurinome und ihre Ergebnisse. *Arch. klin. Chir.*, 1932, 171: 282–325.

530. LIST, C. F. Doppelseitige Medianusneuritis bei Akromegalie. *Dtsch. Z. Nervenheilk.*, 1932, 124: 279–292.

531. LIST, C. F. Die Differentialdiagnose der Kleinhirnbrückenwinkelerkrankungen mit besonderer Berücksichtigung der Tumoren. *Z. ges. Neurol. Psychiat.*, 1933, 144: 54–95.

LIST, C. F. See also No. 300.

LIVINGOOD, L. E. See No. 40.

532. LOCKE, C. E. A review of a year's series of intracranial tumors. *Arch Surg.*, Chicago, Nov. 1921, 3: 560–581.

533. LUGER, A. Zur Kenntnis der im Röntgenbild sichtbaren Hirntumoren mit besonderer Berücksichtigung der Hypophysengangsgeschwülste. *Fortschr. Röntgenstr.*, 1914, 21: 605–614.

MACCALLUM, W. G. See No. 184.

533a. MACCALLUM, W. G., and MCCLURE, R. D. On the mechanical effects of experimental mitral stenosis and insufficiency. *Johns Hopk. Hosp. Bull.*, Aug. 1906, 17: 260–265. Also: *Trans. Ass. Amer. Phys.*, 1906, 21: 5–19.

534. MCCANN, W. S. A study of the carbon dioxide-combining power of the blood plasma in experimental tetany. *J. biol. Chem.*, Sept. 1918, 35: 553–563.

534a. MCCLURE, R. D. An experimental study of intestinal obstruction. *J. Amer. med. Ass.*, Sept. 21, 1907, 49: 1003–1006.

535. MCCLURE, R. D. Hydrocephalus treated by drainage into a vein of the neck. *Johns Hopk. Hosp. Bull.*, April 1909, 20: 110–113.

536. MCCLURE, R. D., and DERGE, H. F. A study of reversal of the intestine. *Johns Hopk. Hosp. Bull.*, Dec. 1907, 18: 472–474.

MCCRAE, T. See Nos. 115, 116, 150, 151, 262, 263.

537. MCIVER, M. A., and HAGGART, W. W. Traumatic shock; some experimental work on crossed circulation. *Surg. Gynec. Obstet.*, April 1923, 36: 542–546.

538. MCKENZIE, K. G. Intrameningeal division of the spinal accessory and roots of the upper cervical nerves for the treatment of spasmodic torticollis. *Surg. Gynec. Obstet.*, July 1924, 39: 5–10.

539. McKenzie, K. G., and Sosman, M. C. The roentgenological diagnosis of craniopharyngeal pouch tumors. *Amer. J. Roentgenol.*, Feb. 1924, 11: 171–176.

540. McLean, A. J. The anuran in bio-titration of pituitrin. *J. Pharmacol.*, July 1928, 33: 301–319.

541. McLean, A. J. The route of absorption of the active principles of the posterior hypophysial lobe. *Endocrinology*, July–Aug. 1928, 12: 467–490.

542. McLean, A. J. Transbuccal approach to the encephalon: in experimental operations upon carnivoral pituitary, pons, and ventral medulla. *Ann. Surg.*, Dec. 1928, 88: 985–993.

543. McLean, A. J. The Bovie electrosurgical current generator. Some underlying principles and results. *Arch. Surg. Chicago*, April 1929, 18: 1863–1873.

544. MacMahon, H. E., Lawrence, J. S., and Maddock, S. J. Experimental obstructive cirrhosis. *Amer. J. Path.*, Nov. 1929, 5: 631–643.

Maddock, C. L. See No. 597.

545. Maddock, S. J., and Trimble, H. C. Prolonged insulin hypoglycemia with symptoms. *J. Amer. med. Ass.*, Sept. 1, 1928, 91: 616–621.

546. Maddock, S. J., and Whitaker, L. R. Effects of sodium tetraiodophenolphthalein in complete biliary obstruction. *Boston med. surg. J.*, May 27, 1926, 194: 973–976.

Maddock, S. J. See also Nos. 380, 544, 620, 621.

547. Mahoney, W. Retrobulbar neuritis due to thallium poisoning from depilatory cream. *J. Amer. med. Ass.*, Feb. 20, 1932, 98: 618–620.

de Martel, T. See No. 4.

548. Martin, P. Le traitement chirurgical des gliomes cavitaires de l'encéphale. *Arch. franco-belg. Chir.*, Sept. 1923, 26: 807–847.

Martin, P. See also Nos. 204, 215, 623.

Marvin, F. W. See No. 434.

549. Meagher, R., and Eisenhardt, L. Intracranial carcinomatous metastases, with note on relation of carcinoma and tubercle. *Ann. Surg.*, Jan. 1931, 93: 132–140.

Meagher, R. See also No. 333.

Milliken, G. See No. 651.

550. Mills, C. W. On the alterations in body temperature

produced in dogs by morphia and ether. *Johns Hopk. Hosp. Bull.,* Dec. 1907, 18: 469–472.

MOORE, R. L. See No. 376.

551. MORELLE, J. Tumors of the acoustic nerve. *Arch. Surg., Chicago,* April 1929, 18: 1886–1895.

552. MOTZFELDT, K. Experimental studies on the relation of the pituitary body to renal function. *J. exp. Med.,* Jan. 1, 1917, 25: 153–188.

MURRAY, H. A. See No. 368.

OCHSNER, A. J. See No. 178.

O'CONOR, V. J. See Nos. 655, 656.

553. ODY, F. Tumors of the basal ganglia. *Arch. Neurol. Psychiat., Chicago,* Feb. 1932, 27: 249–269.

554. OLDBERG, E. Surgical considerations of carcinomatous metastases to the brain. *J. Amer. med. Ass.,* Nov. 4, 1933, 101: 1458–1461.

555. OLDBERG, E. Hemorrhage into gliomas. A review of eight hundred and thirty-two consecutive verified cases of glioma. *Arch. Neurol. Psychiat., Chicago,* Nov. 1933, 30: 1061–1073.

556. OLDBERG, E., and EISENHARDT, L. The neurological diagnosis of tumors of the third ventricle. *Trans. Amer. neurol. Ass.,* 1938, 33–35. Also: Die neurologische Diagnose der Geschwülste des 3. Ventrikels. *Nervenarzt,* 1938, 11: 614–615.

557. OLJENICK, I. Trichlorethylene treatment of trigeminal neuralgia. *J. Amer. med. Ass.,* Oct. 13, 1928, 91: 1085–1087.

558. OLJENICK, I. Parinaud's syndrome. Report of a case of traumatic origin. *Trans. Amer. neurol. Ass.,* 1928, 362–406.

559. OLJENICK, I. Bilateral cervical rib. Clinical and experimental observations on a case. *Arch. Surg., Chicago,* April 1929, 18: 1984–2007.

560. ORTSCHILD, J. F. A report of eight cases of canine neoplasm. *Johns Hopk. Hosp. Bull.,* May 1905, 16: 186–196.

ORTSCHILD, J. F. See also No. 84.

OSLER, W. See Nos. 66, 115, 116, 150, 151, 177, 262, 263.

561. OUGHTERSON, A. W., and POWERS, J. H. The relationship of the toxin of bacillus Welchii to the toxemia of intestinal obstruction. *Arch. Surg., Chicago,* April 1929, 18: 2019–2024.

PEABODY, F. W. See No. 390.

PILCHER, C. See No. 565.

562. POWERS, J. H. The experimental production of mitral stenosis. *Arch. Surg., Chicago*, April 1929, 18: 1945–1959.

563. POWERS, J. H. Experimental cardiac valvular disease in dogs, and subacute and chronic cardiac valvular disease in man. A comparative pathologic study. *Arch. Surg., Chicago*, July 1930, 21: 1–11.

564. POWERS, J. H., BOWIE, M. A., and HOWARD, I. M. Some observations on the blood of normal dogs, with special reference to the total volume. *Amer. J. Physiol.*, April 1930, 92: 665–671.

565. POWERS, J. H., PILCHER, C. and BOWIE, M. A. Some observations on the circulation in experimental mitral stenosis. *Amer. J. Physiol.*, June 1931, 97: 405–411.

POWERS, J. H. See also No. 561.

PUTNAM, I. K. See No. 569.

566. PUTNAM, T. J. Some brominized oils for radiographic use. Preliminary report. *J. Amer. med. Ass.*, Oct. 2, 1926, 87: 1102–1104.

567. PUTNAM, T. J. Separation of growth-promoting hormone from that inducing premature estrus in the anterior pituitary gland. *Arch. Surg., Chicago*, April 1929, 18: 1699–1707.

568. PUTNAM, T. J., BENEDICT, E. B., and TEEL, H. M. Studies in acromegaly. VIII. Experimental canine acromegaly produced by injection of anterior lobe pituitary extract. *Arch. Surg., Chicago*, April 1929, 18: 1708–1736.

569. PUTNAM, T. J., and PUTNAM, I. K. The experimental study of pachymeningitis hemorrhagica. *J. nerv. ment. Dis.*, March 1927, 65: 260–272.

570. PUTNAM, T. J., TEEL, H. M., and BENEDICT, E. B. The preparation of a sterile, active extract from the anterior lobe of the hypophysis. *Amer. J. Physiol.*, Feb. 1928, 84: 157–164.

PUTNAM, T. J. See also Nos. 228, 236, 378, 438, 514, 581, 657, 658.

571. RAND, C. W. A case of supposed progeria (premature senility) in a girl of eight years. *Boston med. surg. J.*, July 16, 1914, 171: 107–111.

REFORD, L. L. See No. 98.

572. RHOADS, C. P., and VAN WAGENEN, W. P. Observations on the histology of the tumors of the nervus acusticus. *Amer. J. Path.*, March 1928, 4: 145–151.

573. RISLEY, E. H. Hemostasis by interposition of muscle, fat and fascia in parenchymatous organs. *Surg. Gynec. Obstet.*, Jan. 1917, 24: 85–89.

ROSSIER, J. See No. 19.

SANDIFORD, I. See Nos. 391, 392, 393.

574. SCARFF, J. E. The experimental production of pulmonary abscess. Etiologic factors. *Arch. Surg.*, Chicago, April 1929, 18: 1960–1983.

575. SCHALTENBRAND, G. Encephalitis periaxialis diffusa (Schilder). A case report with clinical and anatomic studies. *Arch. Neurol. Psychiat.*, Chicago, Dec. 1927, 18: 944–981.

576. SCHALTENBRAND, G. Enthirnungsstarre. Zugleich ein Beitrag zur Theorie der proprioceptiven Lage- und Bewegungsreaktionen. *Dtsch. Z. Nervenheilk.*, 1927, 100: 165–202.

577. SCHALTENBRAND, G. The development of human motility and motor disturbances. *Arch. Neurol. Psychiat.*, Chicago, Oct. 1928, 20: 720–730.

578. SCHALTENBRAND, G. Zur Pathologie der Stellreflexe. *Dtsch. Z. Nervenheilk.*, 1928, 105: 133–176.

579. SCHALTENBRAND, G., and BAILEY, P. Anatomy, physiology and pathology of the perivascular piaglia membrane of the brain. *Trans. Amer. neurol. Ass.*, 1927, 279–280.

580. SCHALTENBRAND, G., and BAILEY, P. Die perivaskuläre Piagliamembran des Gehirns. *J. Psychol. Neurol.*, Lpz., 1928, 35: 199–278.

581. SCHALTENBRAND, G., and PUTNAM, T. J. Untersuchungen zum Kreislauf des Liquor cerebrospinalis mit Hilfe intravenöser Fluorescineinspritzungen. *Dtsch. Z. Nervenheilk.*, 1927, 96: 123–132.

SCHALTENBRAND, G. See also No. 369.

582. SCHLESINGER, B. Syndrome of the fibrillary astrocytomas of the temporal lobe. *Arch. Neurol. Psychiat.*, Chicago, April 1933, 29: 843–854.

583. SCHÖNBAUER, L. Zur operativen Technik der Hirntumoren. *Dtsch. Z. Chir.*, 1925, 191: 343–352.

584. SCHÖNBAUER, L.   Zur Diagnostik und Indikitionsstellung der Tumoren des Grosshirns und des Kleinhirns. *Mitt. Grenzgeb. Med. Chir.*, 1925, 38: 516–524.

585. SCHÖNBAUER, L., and WHITAKER, L. R.   Experimentelle Untersuchungen über den Einfluss des vegetativen Nervensystems auf die Funktion experimentell geschädigter Nieren. *Wien. klin. Wschr.*, 1925, 38: 580–582.

586. SCHÖNBAUER, L., and WHITAKER, L. R.   Experimentelle Untersuchungen über den Einfluss des vegetativen Nervensystems auf die Wundheilung, unter besonderer Berücksichtigung traumatischer Magenläsionen. *Mitt. Grenzgeb. Med. Chir.*, 1925, 38: 500–508.

587. SCHREIBER, F.   Meningioma with bruit: a report of four cases. *New Engl. J. Med.*, Dec. 26, 1929, 201: 1290–1291.

588. SCHREIBER, F.   Intracranial pressure: correlation of choked disc and Roentgen pressure signs. *Amer. J. Roentgenol.*, June 1930, 23: 607–611.

589. SCOTT, W. J. M.   The influence of the adrenal glands on resistance. I. The susceptibility of adrenalectomized rats to morphine. *J. exp. Med.*, Nov. 1923, 38: 543–560.

590. SCOTT, W. J. M.   The influence of the adrenal glands on resistance. II. The toxic effect of killed bacteria in adrenalectomized rats. *J. exp. Med.*, March 1924, 39: 457–471.

591. SCUDDER, C. L., and HARVEY, S. C.   Is the employment of the actual cautery in the treatment of chronic ulcer of the stomach a safe procedure? *Surg. Gynec. Obstet.*, Dec. 1916, 23: 719–724.

592. SHAMOFF, V. N.   Concerning the action of various pituitary extracts upon the isolated intestinal loop. *Amer. J. Physiol.*, Jan. 1916, 39: 268–278.

593. SHAMOFF, V. N.   On the secretory discharge of the pituitary body produced by stimulation of the superior cervical sympathetic ganglion. *Amer. J. Physiol.*, Jan. 1916, 39: 279–290.

SHAMOFF, V. N.   See also No. 394.

594. SIMONS, D. J., and DIONNE, M. J.   The movement of substances in the cerebrospinal fluid. *Proc. Soc. exp. Biol.*, *N.Y.*, March 1931, 28: 669–670.

SLADEN, F. J.   See No. 91.

595. SOSMAN, M. C., WHITAKER, L. R., and EDSON, P. J. Clinical and experimental cholecystography. *Amer. J. Roentgenol.*, Dec. 1925, 14: 495–503.

SOSMAN, M. C. See also Nos. 228, 370, 539.

SPIELMANN, M. H. See No. 242.

596. SPURLING, R. G., and LAWRENCE, J. S. Direct effect of radium irradiation of leukocytes. *Amer. J. med. Sci.*, Feb. 1925, 169: 157–160.

597. SPURLING, R. G., and MADDOCK, C. L. The cerebrospinal fluid in tumor of the brain. *Arch. Neurol. Psychiat.*, *Chicago*, July 1925, 14: 54–63.

598. SPURLING, R. G., and WHITAKER, L. R. End-results of cholecystostomy as shown by the cholecystogram. *Surg. Gynec. Obstet.*, April 1927, 44: 463–467.

599. STATER, W. J. The action of benzyl benzoate and morphine on the vesical sphincter. *J. Urol.*, Sept. 1922, 8: 239–245.

600. STODDARD, J. L., and CUTLER, E. C. Torula infection in man. A group of cases, characterized by chronic lesions of the central nervous system, with clinical symptoms suggestive of cerebral tumor, produced by an organism belonging to the torula group (Torula Histolytica, N. Sp.). *Monogr. Rockefeller Inst. med. Res.*, No. 6, Jan. 31, 1916, 98 pp.

STREETER, E. C. See No. 243.

601. SYMONDS, C. P. Contributions to the clinical study of intracranial aneurysms. I. *Guy's Hosp. Rep.*, April 1923, 73: 139–158.

602. TEEL, H. M. The effects of injecting anterior hypophysial fluid on the course of gestation in the rat. *Amer. J. Physiol.*, Dec. 1926, 79: 170–183.

603. TEEL, H. M. The effects of injecting anterior hypophysial fluid on the production of placentomata in rats. *Amer. J. Physiol.*, Dec. 1926, 79: 184–187.

604. TEEL, H. M. A method for purification of extracts containing the growth-promoting principle of the anterior hypophysis. *Science*, April 12, 1929, 69: 405–406.

605. TEEL, H. M. Diuresis in dogs from neutralized alkaline extracts of the anterior hypophysis. *J. Amer. med. Ass.*, Sept. 7, 1929, 93: 760–761.

606. TEEL, H. M.   The effect of the growth principle of the hypophysis on the female genital tract; with the report of the hypertrophic changes in a case of acromegaly. *Endocrinology,* Nov.–Dec. 1929, 13: 521–528.

607. TEEL, H. M., LEE, M. O., and GAGNON, J.   Basal gaseous metabolism in giant rats. *Proc. Soc. exp. Biol., N.Y.,* Oct. 1929, 27: 23–24.

608. TEEL, H. M., and WATKINS, O.   The effect of extracts containing the growth principle of the anterior hypophysis upon the blood chemistry of dogs. *Amer. J. Physiol.,* Aug. 1929, 89: 662–685.

TEEL, H. M.   See also Nos. 283, 285, 378, 568, 570.

609. THACHER, H. C.   A report of two cases of utero-vaginal prolapse. *Johns Hopk. Hosp. Bull.,* May 1905, 16: 184–186.

THOMAS, H. M.   See Nos. 59, 89.

610. THOMPSON, K. W.   A technique for hypophysectomy of the rat. *Endocrinology,* May–June 1932, 16: 257–263.

611. THOMPSON, K. W.   Inability of sheep to develop antihormone to the gonadotropic hormone from sheep-pituitary glands. *Proc. Soc. exp. Biol., N.Y.,* 1937, 35: 634–637.

612. THOMPSON, K. W.   Non-specificity of thyrotropic antihormone. *Proc. Soc. exp. Biol., N.Y.,* 1937, 35: 637–640.

613. THOMPSON, K. W.   The augmentary factor in animal sera after injections of pituitary extract. *Proc. Soc. exp. Biol., N.Y.,* 1937, 35: 640–644.

614. THOMPSON, K. W.   The principles of endocrine therapy. In: *A System of Therapeutics.* G. Blumer, Ed. New York: D. Appleton-Century Co., 1940, 1: 534–608.

615. THOMPSON, K. W.   Testosterone for the treatment of the eunuchoid state. *Conn. St. med. J.,* Feb. 1939, 3: 59–60.

616. THOMPSON, K. W.   The termination of pregnancy of dogs by gonadotropic antihormone. *Endocrinology,* May 1939.

617. THOMPSON, K. W., and COOMBS, H. I.   The influence of plasmaprotein on the chloride content of the cerebrospinal fluid. *J. exp. Med.,* Sept. 1932, 56: 449–453.

618. THOMPSON, K. W., and DUNPHY, J. E.   Pelvirectal abscess and retroperitoneal cellulitis: report of three cases. *Conn. St. med. J.,* May 1939, 3: 236–238.

619. THOMPSON, K. W., and GAISER, D. W.   The effect of

diet and pituitary growth-hormone on hypophysectomized rats. *Yale J. Biol. Med.*, May 1932, 4: 677–690.

THOMPSON, K. W. See also Nos. 314, 327.

620. TRIMBLE, H. C., and MADDOCK, S. J. A study of the effect of insulin upon the sugar content of erythrocytes, including a comparison of the direct and indirect methods of measurement. *J. biol. Chem.*, July 1928, 78: 323–336.

621. TRIMBLE, H. C., and MADDOCK, S. J. The fluctuations of the capillary blood sugar in normal young men during a twenty-four hour period (including a discussion of the effect of sleep and of mild exercise). *J. biol. Chem.*, March 1929, 81: 595–611.

TRIMBLE, H. C. See also No. 545.

622. VAIL, H. H. Studies by the Bárány rotation and caloric tests of tumors of the nervus acusticus. *Laryngoscope, St. Louis,* Aug. 1920, 30: 505–519.

623. VAN BOGAERT, L., and MARTIN, P. Les tumeurs du quatrième ventricule et le syndrome cérébelleux de la ligne médiane. *Rev. neurol.,* Sept. 1928, 2: 431–483.

624. VAN DESSEL, A. L'incidence et le processus de calcification dans les gliomes du cerveau. *Arch. franco-belg. Chir.,* Oct. 1925, 28: 845–874.

VAN DESSEL, A. See also No. 370.

625. VAN WAGENEN, W. P. Tuberculoma of the brain: its incidence among intracranial tumors and its surgical aspects. *Arch. Neurol. Psychiat., Chicago,* Jan. 1927, 17: 57–91.

626. VAN WAGENEN, W. P. The incidence of intracranial tumors without "choked disk" in one year's series of cases. *Amer. J. med. Sci.,* Sept. 1928, 176: 346–366.

627. VAN WAGENEN, W. P. Verified brain tumors. End results of one hundred and forty-nine cases eight years after operation. *J. Amer. med. Ass.,* May 5, 1934, 102: 1454–1458. See also No. 18 (p. 132–133) and No. 19 (p. 162–164).

VAN WAGENEN, W. P. See also No. 572.

628. VIETS, H. Unilateral ophthalmoplegia. Report of a case due to carotid aneurysm. *J. nerv. ment. Dis.,* April 1918, 47: 249–253.

629. VON GERBER, W. Sarcoma of an undescended testis. *Johns Hopk. Hosp. Bull.,* Dec. 1906, 17: 383–385.

630. WALKER, C. B. Some new perimetry instruments. *J. Amer. med. Ass.*, July 26, 1913, 61: 277.

631. WALKER, C. B. Topical diagnostic value of the hemiopic pupillary reaction and the Wilbrand hemianoptic prism phenomenon, with a new method of performing the latter. *J. Amer. med. Ass.*, Sept. 27, 1913, 61: 1152–1156.

632. WALKER, C. B. Some new instruments for measuring visual-field defects. *Arch. Ophthal., N.Y.*, 1913, 42: 577–591.

633. WALKER, C. B. Further observations on the hemiopic pupillary reaction obtained with a new clinical instrument. *J. Amer. med. Ass.*, Sept. 5, 1914, 63: 846–851.

634. WALKER, C. B. Observations on the topical diagnostic and psychiatrical value of the Wilbrand test with a new clinical instrument. *Arch. Ophthal., N.Y.*, Feb. 1915, 44: 109–128.

635. WALKER, C. B. A contribution to the study of bitemporal hemianopsia with new instruments and methods for detecting slight changes. *Arch. Ophthal., N.Y.*, July 1915, 44: 369–402.

636. WALKER, C. B. A new instrument for deep sewing. *J. Amer. med. Ass.*, March 3, 1917, 68: 707–708.

637. WALKER, C. B. Quantitative perimetry: Practical devices and errors. *Arch. Ophthal., N.Y.*, Nov. 1917, 46: 537–561.

638. WALKER, C. B. Neurologic perimetry and a method of imitating daylight with electric illumination. *Trans. Amer. med. Ass.*, 1917, 189–202.

639. WALKER, C. B. The value of quantitative perimetry in the study of postethmoidal sphenoidal sinusitis causing visual defects. *Boston med. surg. J.*, Sept. 15, 1921, 185: 321–326.

WALKER, C. B. See also Nos. 124, 146, 160, 167.

WATKINS, O. See No. 608.

640. WEED, L. H. Studies on the cerebrospinal fluid. II. The theories of drainage of cerebrospinal fluid with an analysis of the methods of investigation. *J. med. Res.*, Sept. 1914, 31: 21–49.

641. WEED, L. H. Studies on the cerebrospinal fluid. III. The pathways of escape from the subarachnoid spaces

with particular reference to the arachnoid villi. *J. med. Res.,* Sept. 1914, 31: 51–91.

642. WEED, L. H.   Studies on the cerebrospinal fluid. IV. The dual source of cerebrospinal fluid. *J. med. Res.,* Sept. 1914, 31: 93–117.

WEED, L. H.   See also Nos. 125, 143, 153, 645.

643. WEGEFARTH, P.   Studies on the cerebrospinal fluid. V. The drainage of intraocular fluids. *J. med. Res.,* Sept. 1914, 31: 119–147.

644. WEGEFARTH, P.   Studies on the cerebrospinal fluid. VI. The establishment of drainage of intraocular and intracranial fluids into the venous system. *J. med. Res.,* Sept. 1914, 31: 149–166.

645. WEGEFARTH, P., and WEED, L. H.   Studies on the cerebrospinal fluid. VII. Analogous processes of the cerebral and ocular fluids. *J. med. Res.,* Sept. 1914, 31: 167–176.

646. WHITAKER, L. R.   A case of chronic tuberculous meningitis simulating brain tumor. *Amer. Rev. Tuberc.,* May 1925, 11: 175–183.

647. WHITAKER, L. R.   The mechanism of the gall bladder. *Amer. J. Physiol.,* Oct. 1926, 78: 411–436.

648. WHITAKER, L. R.   The mechanism of the gall bladder and its relation to cholelithiasis. *J. Amer. med. Ass.* May, 14, 1927, 88: 1542–1548.

649. WHITAKER, L. R.   Diagnosis of gall bladder disease. Application of recent advances in physiology. *J. Amer. med. Ass.,* June 4, 1927, 88: 1791–1796.

650. WHITAKER, L. R.   Problems in normal and in abnormal physiology of the gallbladder. *Arch. Surg., Chicago,* April 1929, 18: 1783–1802.

651. WHITAKER, L. R., and MILLIKEN, G.   A comparison of sodium tetrabromphenolphthalein with sodium tetraiodophenolphthalein in gall-bladder radiography. *Surg. Gynec. Obstet.,* Jan. 1925, 40: 17–23.

WHITAKER, L. R.   See also Nos. 443, 444, 519, 546, 585, 586, 595, 598.

652. WISLOCKI, G. B.   Observations on "Dioctophyme Renale" in dogs. *J. Parasit.,* Dec. 1919 (issued 1920), 6: 94–97.

653. WISLOCKI, G. B.   Experimental studies on fetal absorp-

tion. I. The vitally stained fetus. II. The behavior of the fetal membranes and placenta of the cat toward colloidal dyes injected into the maternal blood-stream. *Contr. Embryol. Carneg. Instn.*, 1920, 11: 45–60.

654. WISLOCKI, G. B., and KEY, J. A. The distribution of mitochondria in the placenta. *Contr. Embryol. Carneg. Instn.*, 1921, 13: 103–115.

655. WISLOCKI, G. B., and O'CONOR, V. J. Experimental observations upon the ureters, with especial reference to peristalsis and antiperistalsis. *Johns Hopk. Hosp. Bull.*, June 1920, 31: 197–202.

656. WISLOCKI, G. B. and O'CONOR, V. J. Experimental observations upon the ureter. *Amer. J. Physiol.*, March 1921, 55: 316–317.

657. WISLOCKI, G. B. and PUTNAM, T. J. Note on the anatomy of the areae postremae. *Anat. Rec.*, Oct. 1920, 19: 281–287.

658. WISLOCKI, G. B. and PUTNAM, T. J. Absorption from the ventricles in experimentally produced internal hydrocephalus. *Amer. J. Anat.*, Sept. 1921, 29: 313–320.

WOLBACH, S. B. See Nos. 252, 371.

V. APPENDIX

APPENDIX A

ASSISTANTS IN NEUROLOGICAL SURGERY

George J. Heuer	1908–1909: Asst. res. surg.
Samuel J. Crowe	1909–1910: Asst. res. surg.
Emil Goetsch	1910–1911: Asst. res. surg.
William Sharpe	1911–1911: Asst. res. surg.
Walter E. Dandy	1911–1912: Asst. res. surg.
Howard A. Naffziger	1912–1913: Asst. res. surg.
Charles Bagley, Jr.	Jan. 1913–Jan. 1914: Asst. res. surg.
Carl W. Rand	Oct. 1913–Nov. 1914: Asst. res. surg.
Edward B. Towne	Nov. 1914–Nov. 1915: Asst. res. surg.
Clifford B. Walker	March 1915–April 1918: Assoc. in surg.
Gilbert Horrax	Nov. 1915–Nov. 1916: Asst. res. surg.; 1919–1928, Assoc. in surg.; 1928–1932, Sr. Assoc. in surg.
Samuel C. Harvey	Nov. 1916–May 1917: Asst. res. surg.
Percival Bailey	April–Dec. 1919: Asst. res. surg.; 1922–1925, Jr. Assoc. in surg.; 1926–1928, Assoc. in surg.
Howard Fleming	Dec. 1919–June 1920: Asst. res. surg.
Charles E. Locke, Jr.	June 1920–June 1921: Asst. res. surg.
Daniel W. Wheeler	June 1921–March 1922: Asst. res. surg.
Paul Martin	Sept. 1921–Nov. 1922: Asst. res. surg.
Kenneth G. McKenzie	Nov. 1922–Nov. 1923: Asst. res. surg.
James P. Ross	April–Sept. 1923: Jr. Assoc. in surg.
Tracy J. Putnam	Nov. 1923–Oct. 1924: Asst. res. surg.
W. P. Van Wagenen	Oct. 1924–Oct. 1925: Asst. res. surg.
Norman M. Dott	Nov. 1923–June 1924: Jr. Assoc. in surg.
Loyal E. Davis	March–Oct. 1924: Jr. Assoc. in surg.
Leo M. Davidoff	Nov. 1925–Oct. 1926: Asst. res. surg.
Hugh W. B. Cairns	Oct. 1926–Sept. 1927: Asst. res. surg.
Claude S. Beck	April–June 1927: Asst. res. surg.
Arthur J. McLean	Sept. 1927–June 1928: Asst. res. surg.
Louise Eisenhardt	March 1928–Nov. 1934: Jr. Assoc. in surg.
John F. Fulton	March–June 1928: Jr. Assoc. in surg.
John E. Scarff	July 1928–July 1929: Asst. res. surg.
Frederic Schreiber	Oct. 1928–Aug. 1929: Asst. res. surg.
Richard C. Buckley	Nov. 1928–Nov. 1929: Jr. Assoc. in surg.
Eric Oldberg	Oct. 1929–Oct. 1930: Asst. res. surg.
Norman M. Dott	July–Aug. 1929: Acting asst. res. surg.
Richard H. Meagher	Nov. 1929–May 1930: Asst. res. surg.
William R. Henderson	May 1930–July 1931: Asst. res. surg.
Hugh W. B. Cairns	Sept. 5–19, 1930: Acting asst. res. surg.
Thomas I. Hoen	Oct. 1930–Sept. 1931: Asst. res. surg.
William deG. Mahoney	March 1931–April 1932: Asst. res. surg.
Bronson S. Ray	Oct. 1931–Sept. 1932: Asst. res. surg.
Richard U. Light	April 1932–Aug. 1932: Asst. res. surg.

APPENDIX B

APPOINTEES IN THE "OLD HUNTERIAN" AT THE JOHNS HOPKINS MEDICAL SCHOOL AND THE ARTHUR TRACY CABOT FELLOWS IN CHARGE OF THE LABORATORY OF SURGICAL RESEARCH AT HARVARD

Philip K. Gilman	1905–06	George B. Wislocki	1919–20
J. Frank Ortschild	1906–07	Percival Bailey	1920–21
Lewis L. Reford	1907–08	Roger C. Graves	1921–22
Samuel J. Crowe	1908–09	W. J. Merle Scott	1922–23
Emil Goetsch	1909–10	Claude S. Beck	1923–24
Walter E. Dandy	1910–11	Lester R. Whitaker	1924–25
Conrad Jacobson	1911–12	Tracy J. Putnam	1925–26
Lewis H. Weed	1912–14	Arthur J. McLean	1926–27
Gilbert Horrax	1914–15	John H. Powers	1927–28
Samuel C. Harvey	1915–16	Harold M. Teel	1928–29
William S. McCann	1916–17	Paul Martin	1929–30
George B. Wislocki	1917–18	Richard H. Meagher	1930–31
[No appointee]	1918–19	Richard U. Light	1931–32

APPOINTEES TO THE SURGICAL LABORATORY OF THE PETER BENT BRIGHAM HOSPITAL

Percival Bailey 1922–28   Richard C. Buckley 1928–29

Louise Eisenhardt 1929–33

APPENDIX C

VOLUNTARY GRADUATE ASSISTANTS

Charles P. Symonds, London	June–Sept. 1920
Frédéric Bremer, Brussels	Oct. 1920–April 1921
Ferdinand C. Lee, Baltimore	June–Sept. 1923
Leopold Schönbauer, Vienna	Nov. 1924–Jan. 1925
Arthur Van Dessel, Louvain	Feb.–July 1925
Boris M. Fried, Boston	1925–1932
Jean Morelle, Louvain	Oct. 1925–June 1926
Francis C. Grant, Philadelphia	Oct. 1925–May 1926
Walter Lehmann, Göttingen	Jan.–April 1926
Edgar F. Fincher, Jr., Atlanta	June–Sept. 1926
Georges Schaltenbrand, Hamburg	June 1926–March 1927
Ignatius Oljenick, Amsterdam	March 1927–March 1929
Frederick E. Kredel, Baltimore	June–Sept. 1927; id. 1928
John F. Fulton, New Haven	July 1927–March 1928
Cyril B. Courville, Los Angeles	Aug. 1927–Jan. 1928
Lawrence S. Kubie, New York	Sept.–Oct. 1927
Dimitri Bagdasar, Bucarest	Oct. 1927–Oct. 1928
Alan C. Gairdner, London	Nov. 1928–Jan. 1929
Edwin M. Deery, New York	Nov. 1928–Sept. 1929
Attracta Halpenny, Dublin	Sept.–Dec. 1929
Gaston De Coppet, Bern	Sept. 1929–Aug. 1930
F. A. R. Stammers, Birmingham	Oct.–Nov. 1929
George Armitage, Leeds	Nov. 1929–Nov. 1930
Daniel Petit-Dutaillis, Paris	April–June 1930
Donald C. Bell, Cleveland	Nov.–Dec. 1930
François Ody, Geneva	Nov. 1930–Sept. 1931
Alexander Zeitlin, Rostov	Dec. 1930–Jan. 1931
Carl F. List, Berlin	March 1931–March 1932
Benno Schlesinger, Vienna	May 1931–May 1932
Abraham Kaplan, New York	July 1931–June 1932
Robert A. Groff, Philadelphia	Oct. 1931–June 1932
Johannes Rives, Tartu	Dec. 1931
Alfred R. D. Pattison, Newcastle	March–Oct. 1932
D. Vasiliu, Bucarest	April–Aug. 1932
Arist A. Stender, Hamburg	May–Aug. 1932
Ferdinand Verbeek, Groningen	June–Aug. 1932

APPENDIX D

THE HARVEY CUSHING SOCIETY

HONORARY MEMBERS

*Harvey Cushing, New Haven. Ernest Sachs, St. Louis.

CORRESPONDING MEMBERS

Hugh W. B. Cairns, Oxford.
Otfrid Foerster, Breslau.
Geoffrey Jefferson, Manchester.

Thierry de Martel, Paris.
Herbert Olivecrona, Stockholm.
Clovis Vincent, Paris.

ACTIVE MEMBERS

Gilbert Anderson, New Orleans.
Percival Bailey, Chicago.
Richard M. Brickner, New York.
Paul C. Bucy, Chicago.
Eldridge H. Campbell, Albany.
W. E. Chamberlain, Philadelphia.
W. McK. Craig, Rochester, Minn.
Albert S. Crawford, Detroit.
W. Gayle Crutchfield, Richmond.
Leo M. Davidoff, Brooklyn.
Albert D'Errico, Dallas.
Cornelius G. Dyke, New York.
Louise Eisenhardt, New Haven.
Temple Fay, Philadelphia.
Edgar F. Fincher, Jr., Atlanta.
John F. Fulton, New Haven.
William J. German, New Haven.
Nicholas Gotten, Memphis
Hale A. Haven, Seattle.
Gilbert Horrax, Boston.
Franc D. Ingraham, Boston.
Franklin Jelsma, Louisville.
Edgar A. Kahn, Ann Arbor.
* Deceased.

Roland M. Klemme, St. Louis.
Lawrence S. Kubie, New York.
Richard U. Light, Kalamazoo.
Walter I. Lillie, Philadelphia.
J. G. Love, Rochester, Minn.
J. G. Lyerly, Jacksonville.
Kenneth G. McKenzie, Toronto.
Eric Oldberg, Chicago.
Cobb Pilcher, Nashville.
James L. Poppen, Boston.
Tracy J. Putnam, New York.
F. L. Reichert, San Francisco.
Lawrence Reynolds, Detroit.
Frederic Schreiber, Detroit.
R. Eustace Semmes, Memphis.
Merrill C. Sosman, Boston.
Ernest Spiegel, Philadelphia.
R. Glen Spurling, Louisville.
Frank R. Teachenor, Kansas City.
Frank Turnbull, Vancouver.
W.P.Van Wagenen, Rochester, N.Y.
James W. Watts, Washington.
James C. White, Boston.
Harry Wilkins, Oklahoma City.

VI. SUBJECT INDEX

INDEX

Numerals refer to the numbered entries of the bibliography, not to pages.

VII. ADDENDUM

CUSHING AT THE BRIGHAM

A PHOTOGRAPHIC ESSAY

RICHARD U. LIGHT

PHOTO CREDITS:

Numbers 7, 10, 13, 14, 15, and 17 were taken
by Dr. Walter W. Boyd, a Brigham house officer.

The others were made by Dr. Light.

1.
THE HOSPITAL

Peter Bent Brigham, a Boston fish peddler-turned-financier, left a fortune for the building of a charity hospital, which fulfilled Harvard's need for a university hospital located close to its medical school. The hospital opened for patients in January, 1913, and served until 1975 when construction of the Brigham and Women's Hospital was begun. Only the handsome porticoed entrance and administrative center, shown here, have survived from the original structure.

The Brigham was small by hospital standards, two hundred fifty beds, half medical, half surgical. Henry Christian was Chief of Medicine, Harvey Cushing Chief of Surgery. With its research laboratories and clinical teaching facilities, it followed the lead set by the Johns Hopkins Hospital in Baltimore.

2.
GREETINGS FROM THE CHIEF

3.
THE OFFICE

Dr. Cushing's office was situated under the operating rooms. There were two ways of getting in to see him, one guarded by his secretary, the other shown here which gave direct access from the hall, and was often used by his staff, for he was surprisingly accessible and seemingly undisturbed by interruptions.

4.
AT THE DESK

5.

THE SURGICAL STAFF

A group photograph of the surgical staff was taken May, 1930, when the noted Swedish surgeon, Dr. Gunnar Nyström, was serving as Cushing's *locum tenens.*

Front Row: Richard Light, Donald Dial, Richard Farnsworth, Tom Hoen, Louise Eisenhardt, William Mahoney, Ted Scarff

Second Row: Harlan Newton, Gilbert Horrax, John Homans, Gunnar Nyström, Cushing, David Cheever, Francis Newton, John Powers (Resident in Surgery)

Top Row: Kenneth Thompson, John Lawrence, Frederick A. Fender, Bronson Ray, William Green (Resident in Surgery), Eric Oldberg, George Armitage (Leeds), William Henderson (Edinborough), Richard Meagher, Edward Castle.

Two men in the background are not identified.

6.
THE INSTRUMENTS

The collection of hemostats, scissors, scalpels, rongeurs, forceps, retractors, drills, even a brace and bit—the tools of the neurosurgeon's trade in the 1920's.

Cushing used a set of hand signals to indicate what he wanted handed to him by the instrument man: the thumb and forefinger pinched for a scalpel, an open palm for the needle holder, rapid motion of two fingers for scissors, etc.

The use of hand signals removed the possibility of wound contamination from talking, and enabled the surgeon to concentrate on the field of operation without looking up to pick out an instrument.

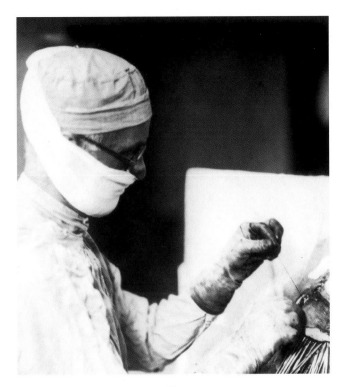

7.
THE KNOT

One of Halsted's innovations was the use of fine silk thread for sutures and ligatures, and Cushing is seen here inserting a row of interrupted silk sutures during the closure of the wound. The thread was wound on a nine inch board, and cut into eighteen inch suture lengths and lightly waxed.

It took months of practice on a bedpost learning to tie knots rapidly, first a granny knot that can be slipped to a tight position in a deep hole, followed by a square knot to prevent loosening.

8.
THE SKETCH

Following the operation, Cushing would retreat to the dressing room to dictate the operative note, and to sketch the salient points of the operation, often in two or three drawings. Still robed in gown and gloves, he would have tea and toast before returning to the operating room to do the dressings on earlier patients.

In 1992 the American Association of Neurological Surgeons published a handsome volume of Cushing's sketches under the title "The Surgical Art of Harvey Cushing". It was compiled by six neurologists and neurosurgeons of the Brigham and Women's Hospital under the editorship of Peter McL. Black.

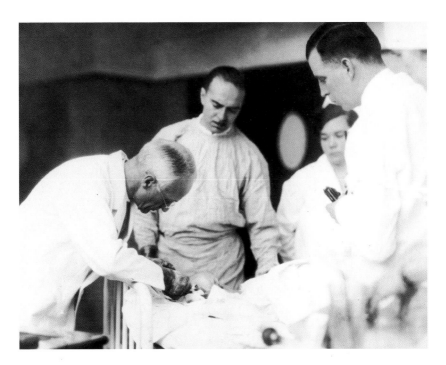

9.
POSTOPERATIVE CARE

The morning operation finished and the room cleaned up, Dr. Cushing returned to examine the wounds of his recovering patients.

The two men standing by were Voluntary Graduate Assistants, Gaston De Coppet from Berne, Switzerland, and George Armitage from Leeds, England. These Graduate Assistants gained almost as much experience as did the Residents (Cushing's residents did no major surgery on their own), and their case histories and follow-ups appear on the typed hospital records alongside those of the Resident. They did not scrub, however, and watched the operation from a moveable stand. For those with extensive experience in general surgery, a month or two of observation was sufficient to learn Cushing's methods of neurosurgery, as it was for Herbert Olivecrona who returned to Stockholm to establish one of the best neurosurgical operative clinics in Europe. The men pictured here, on the other hand, stayed a full year. (Continued on next page.)

Cushing's Residents (actually listed as Assistant Residents on the hospital's roster as well as on its payroll) were the hardest working men on the team, and those who held the post during the mid-20s as Cushing's career rose to its peak were sorely tried. From Van Wagenen in 1924 on through Norman Dott, Loyal Davis, Leo Davidoff to Hugh Cairns in 1926-27, the work load grew steadily heavier. Cairns, an Australian veteran of World War I, confessed to Fulton that Gallipoli and the Battle of the Marne were as nothing compared to the clinical stress of a year as Cushing's neurosurgical resident. He operated all day, and in the evenings did dressings, examined patients, and dictated detailed histories; if four or five hours of uninterrupted sleep were obtained in a night, he could count himself fortunate. (Cushing later eased the situation by appointing two men to the post.)

Fortunate was the resident who had a sense of humor and could match wits with his chief. One day in the midst of an operation, Cushing paused and said: "Cairns, you've been smoking. I can always tell a man who smokes." To which Cairns quietly replied "And can you tell the brand?"

Afterwards Cairns established himself as one of the leading neurosurgeons in England, held the first Nuffield Professorship in Surgery at Oxford, and a Baronetcy followed.

10.
CONFERENCE AT THE BEDSIDE

S. Burt Wolbach, pathologist; Richard Pearson Strong, tropical medicine; William Henry Welch, pathologist, hygienist and Harvey Cushing. Welch was from Johns Hopkins, the others from Harvard.

11.
THREE SURGEONS

Dr. David Cheever on the left was senior among the general surgeons at the Brigham. At the right was Dr. René Leriche of Strasbourg, France. He had come to the United States to attend a surgical congress and to receive an honorary degree from Harvard, and stayed to spend a week as Surgeon-in-Chief *pro tempore* at the Brigham. Of this Cushing wrote: "He entered with great spirit into the institutional life of the hospital interns, and it is most pleasant to feel that we have established contact with the celebrated Alsatian Clinic which our graduates during their travels abroad will be certain to visit in the years to come." (1929)

12.
CUSHING AND PAVLOV

In August, 1929, the aging Pavlov, he of the conditioned reflex, came over from Russia to attend the Thirteenth International Physiological Congress in Boston. While here he spent a day watching a Cushing operation which proved difficult for the surgeon because Pavlov scorned the face mask, and became so excited that he nearly pushed his prominent whiskers into the wound.

13.
CUSHING AND FOERSTER

Otfrid Foerster arrived from Breslau, Germany in October, 1930, to act as Surgeon-in-Chief *pro tempore*. A gentle, friendly man, he endeared himself to the hospital family. Although he was one of Europe's leading neurologists, he took up surgery very late, perhaps under compulsion. A visitor to his clinic the following summer found that he had reverted to the nineteenth century German operating room garb of rubber boots and a rubber apron for protection against expected heavy bleeding!! (Cushing's team wore white shoes.)

14.
CUSHING, SVEN HEDIN AND HIS SISTER ALMA

Sven Hedin was the noted Swedish explorer of the Gobi Desert in North China. On one of these trips he began suffering headaches and returned to Peking where he was seen by Cushing's former pupil, Georges Schaltenbrand who, fearing a brain tumor, sent him on to Boston. Fortunately there was no evidence of tumor, but the Hedins remained in Boston a week or more to the great delight of the Cushings with whom a warm friendship developed.

15.
PUTTI AND CUSHING EXAMINE A RARE BOOK

The Italian surgeon Vittorio Putti served as Surgeon-in-Chief, *pro tempore* in June, 1932, and Cushing recorded the event: "As all orthopaedists know, Professor Putti is a bachelor who lives and conducts his celebrated clinic in a most picturesque XVIth century Benedictine Monastery known as S. Michele in Bosco overlooking this ancient city of Bologna where the university idea had its birth. That he was willing to change his comfortable abode in this quiet sylvan retreat for a cot in the residents' quarters facing the noisiest street corner in Boston was a tribute not only to the Brigham, but to the Children's Hospital as well. He is a student of medical history, a bibliophile and a scholar whose charming personality will not easily be forgotten by the young men who were privileged to come in contact with him as a co-worker."

16.
THE DOCTOR AND HIS BOOKS

"There is only one thing to do with a young man: place both books and cigarettes in his way and caution him to beware of them as dangerous habits. He'll certainly take to one, and perhaps both.

"This may after all be the right tack—to warn young people against books. Or at least against book-collecting; for one may easily become enslaved and soon so enveloped by books that they are on the floor and out in the front hall and in the dining room till you never can find the volume you want and feel sure your wife or the children must have taken it from the place you last put it, when they borrowed your paste pot and scissors."

Cushing's own collection—"the finest collection of medical books gathered by an individual since John Hunter willed his to the University of Glasgow in 1783"—was left to Yale to be joined later on by Fulton's collection and that of Klebs.

17.
CUSHING WITH HIS SWEDISH GUEST,
GUNNAR NYSTRÖM

In May, 1930 Nyström acted as Surgeon-in-Chief *pro tempore* at the Brigham Hospital. Nyström's good nature and his willingness to get up and operate at all hours, gave a big lift to the members of the junior house staff with whom he lived.

18.
CUSHING AND SOSMAN

Before the days of imaging with scan, magnetic resonance and echo sounding, roentgenology of the brain, even with the help of ventriculography, was often based on faint clues. Whenever during an operation it became evident that the x-ray diagnosis was wrong, its perpetrator was summarily called to the operating room to witness the rest of the operation. Small wonder then that Sosman soon became the pre-eminent neuroradiologist of his time!

Merrill Sosman was the leading prankster of the Brigham and one staff member after another fell victim to his traps. Just what he had on Cushing at this moment we do not know, but he seems to have been rendered speechless.

"Die Alpenketten" Berne Septr 1901
Harvey Cushing
William H. Welch sieht die Jungfrau en.

19.
CUSHING AND WELCH

Taken during the First International Neurological Congress in Berne, Switzerland, September, 1931. The Congress was the occasion of Cushing's final public report of his brain tumor mortality statistics, and it aroused great interest. Over 25 of his former pupils attended, fifteen from Europe, and several coming over from the United States. Welch, that marvelous old raconteur, was everywhere, and the last to bed after spinning his captivating yarns all evening to the impressionable youngsters who were foolish enough to believe them. This picture of the two old friends is notable for its timing, for it was taken in the twilight of their careers. (Welch died three years later at the age of 84.)

20.
ARNOLD KLEBS

No story of Cushing's Brigham years would be complete without the mention of Arnold Klebs. Swiss born and fluent in four languages, son of the famous co-discoverer of the diphtheria bacillus, Klebs was host and advisor to many friends made during his American days as Director of the Chicago Tuberculosis Institute (1896–1909). Married to a wealthy American woman, he retired to a charming terraced villa on Lake Geneva to collect and study the scientific manuscripts of the 15th century. From the early twenties on, Cushing and Welch were often summertime guests at Les Terrasses, and were taken by Klebs on automobile excursions into neighboring parts of France and Italy and Austria. Nor should one forget that Klebs made a surprise appearance at Cushing's 70th birthday party in New Haven, and that it was then perhaps that those arch conspirators, Fulton and Cushing, mesmerized him into leaving his treasured collection of over 14,000 volumes to Yale upon his death.

Klebs is pictured on the hotel balcony at Berne during the First International Neurological Congress in September, 1931. The evening before he had hosted a magnificent dinner for 40 in honor of Welch and Cushing.

21.
WILLIAM P. VAN WAGENEN, FIRST PRESIDENT
OF THE HARVEY CUSHING SOCIETY

The formation of the Cushing Society filled the need of a grow-ing number of young neurosurgeons for a forum in which to share experiences and ideas, and to cement the collegiate friendships so important to professionals.

The leaders of this movement were William P. Van Wagenen of Rochester, New York, and Glen Spurling of Louisville, who approached Cushing for permission to use his name for the new Society. He gave his consent, no doubt secretly pleased with the compliment. Papers were signed in Cushing's office in the spring of 1931, and the first meeting was scheduled for May, 1932, in Boston with Van Wagenen as President and Spurling as Vice-President.

(Photographed in Van Wagenen's office in the Strong Memorial Hospital, 1933.)

In its early years the Harvey Cushing Society was more of a club than a serious scientific society. True, papers were read and the host member staged an operation which the others gathered around to watch, but the small numbers made home entertainment possible and many close friendships developed. Promising applicants were invited to a meeting, and if found socially acceptable were invited to the next meeting and elected to membership. But soon this growing Society reached its limit of 35 and the size was increased to 50; the cycle was repeated, and the idea of a limited membership was abandoned altogether, necessitating some better form of selection, so in 1940 the American Board of Neurological Surgery was born. There followed the *Journal of Neurosurgery,* the first issue of which appeared in January, 1944. The Society had now fulfilled the principal functions of such an organization, namely, to keep up membership records and arrange meetings, to establish accreditation procedures, and to publish a journal. That this small group could have accomplished all that in little more than a decade attests to the quality of its leadership in those early days.

Over the years other neurosurgical societies have appeared: regional, international, a Congress, but the Cushing Society has remained the leader, and in 1965 with around 900 members the name was changed to The American Association of Neurological Surgeons. Now in 1993, with a membership of nearly 3,700 drawn from all parts of the globe, the term "American" seems too restrictive, and another name change is being discussed, perhaps a return to its first title in honoring anew the most worldly figure of this surgical century.

22.
*CHARTER MEMBERS OF THE HARVEY CUSHING
SOCIETY, 1932*

Original members at the first meeting held at the Peter Bent Brigham Hospital, May 6, 1932.

Back Row: R. Glen Spurling, R. Eustace Semmes, Temple Fay, Eric Oldberg, Stafford Warren*, William J. German, W. Edward Chamberlain, J.G. Lyerly, Merrill C. Sosman, William P. Van Wagenen, Frank Fremont-Smith*, Leo M. Davidoff, Roland M. Klemme, Frank R. Teachenor. *Guests.

Front Row: Edgar A. Kahn, Paul C. Bucy, Franc D. Ingraham, Louise Eisenhardt, John F. Fulton, Tracy J. Putnam, Franklin Jelsma.

Missing from picture: Gilbert Anderson, Edgar R. Fincher, W.J. Gardner and Frederic Schreiber.

23.
FIFTEEN YEARS LATER AT HOT SPRINGS, VIRGINIA

The charter members attending this fifteenth meeting of the Society, held November 14, 1947, are lined up in approximately the same order.

Back Row: R. Glen Spurling, R. Eustace Semmes, Temple Fay, W. Edward Chamberlain, James G. Lyerly, William P. Van Wagenen, Leo M. Davidoff, Roland M. Klemme and Frederic Schreiber.

Front Row: Edgar A. Kahn, Paul C. Bucy, Franc D. Ingraham, Louise Eisenhardt, Tracy J. Putnam, Franklin Jelsma and Gilbert Anderson.

Missing from picture: Eric Oldberg, William J. German, Merrill C. Sosman, Frank R. Teachenor, John F. Fulton, Edgar R. Fincher, and W.J. Gardner.

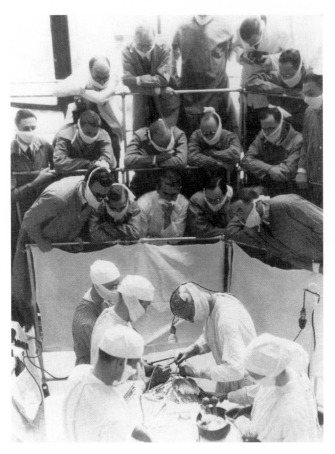

24.
THE HARVEY CUSHING SOCIETY IN THE VIEWING STAND

The inaugural meeting of the Harvey Cushing Society took place in Boston, May 6, 1932. Sixteen members crowded into the moveable stand to watch Cushing operate.

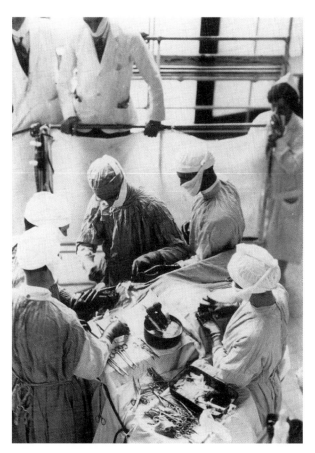

25.
THE 2,000TH BRAIN TUMOR OPERATION

This occurred on April 15, 1932, just four months before Cushing's retirement. The tumor was a chromophile adenoma, which he handled with little difficulty. Following the operation, Dr. Homans presented him with a silver cigarette box from the surgical staff, and read a telegram sent from Detroit: "Have learned that your 2,000th has just come off the line. I drove my 20 millionth off yesterday—you must add four zeros.
—Henry."

Two movie cameras recorded the operation, and videotape copies may be obtained from the AANS headquarters.

26.
CUTLER AND CUSHING

On September 1, 1932, Elliott Cutler took over from Cushing as Moseley Professor of Surgery at Harvard and Surgeon-in-Chief at the Peter Bent Brigham Hospital. He was a general surgeon with little interest in neurosurgery, which went into decline until revived by Franc Ingraham and Donald Matson who added the Brigham to their work at the Children's Hospital.

For Richard Light
"perpetrator"
from JTC
"victim"
PBBH June 30 '33 Temp 96°

27.
CUSHING IN RETIREMENT

There is sadness in this picture, for it shows the plight of the man of action, the conquistador come home after 37 years in the surgical saddle, honored and bemedalled, but shorn of all armor except the inkpot and the pen.

Unprepared for retirement, Cushing used a room in the laboratory area for writing, a depressingly hot, airless room furnished with a chair and a table. Here he remained for nearly a year.

Harvard showed little interest in keeping him, offering only a title that would be meaningless without institutional support, and $1,700 a year, the salary of an instructor. Three others though were in active pursuit: Western Reserve, Johns Hopkins, and Yale. He procrastinated all winter and finally, in mid-June, accepted Yale's offer of a Sterling Professorship backed up with a secretary and generous office space.

The Cushing family moved to New Haven in October, 1933.

28.
PROFESSOR AND PUPIL

John Fulton, Sterling Professor of Physiology at Yale, was a man of many talents. In addition to teaching, he conducted research in the neurophysiology of animals closest to man (the apes: gibbons, orangutans, chimpanzees, and gorillas) in his Primate Research Laboratory. A Rhodes Scholar and a Harvard medical graduate, he served as one of Cushing's Voluntary Graduate Assistants and was part of the group that formed the Harvey Cushing Society. Cushing named him to be his literary executor, and he wrote the definitive biography of the man he admired so much.

29.
CUSHING AND A DISTANT COUSIN

At the fourth meeting of the Harvey Cushing Society held in New Haven, May 1935, John Fulton brought out one of his favorite primates to meet the crowd. Dr. Cushing shared in the fun.

The Fulton home was a spacious house atop Mill Rock, overlooking the city of New Haven. After the death of John and his wife, Lucia, it was purchased by the Axion Foundation to house the Fulton-Cushing Collection and Museum, thus furthering Yale's dedication to medical history—a subject close to the hearts of both Cushing and his devoted protégé.

30.

HARVEY • CUSHING
MOSELEY • PROFESSOR • OF
SURGERY • MCMXII • MCMXXXII

It seems appropriate to conclude this review of "Cushing at the Brigham" with the medal celebrating his 20 years as Harvard's Chief surgeon, designed by a dentist-turned-sculptor named Paul Adrian Brodeur. The plaque shown here is an acrylic copy of the plaster cast, measuring 10" by 15", from which the dies of the medal were cut through a reduction process.

In 1970 the writer entered a taxicab at Boston's airport and said, "Take me to 721 Huntington Avenue." The driver corrected him: "You mean the Peter Bent Brigham Hospital where Dr. Harvey Cushing used to operate."

They still remembered!